D1518702

WARRIORS
IN
RECOVERY

Women who stood up to addiction and won the damn battle

A book of hope and inspiration for women in addiction and women who love someone with addiction.

MELANIE MOBERG

Keri,
Enjoy each
everyday you are given.
Melanie

DISCLAIMER

At any point, if you are struggling with thoughts of suicide, do not hesitate to call the Suicide Prevention Hotline at 1-800-273-8255 or text the crisis line at 741741. You are never alone and you are loved.

If you are experiencing physical violence or abuse, please reach out for help. No one deserves to be hurt in any way. If you need support, please call the Domestic Violence Abuse Hotline at 1-800-799-7233 or chat online at thehotline.org.

The purpose of this book is solely to provide educational information and share the author's personal opinions and experiences. It is for informational purposes only. The information and resources contained in this book are not intended to assess, diagnose, or treat any medical and/or mental health condition. Please seek professional assistance as needed. The author disclaims any liability in connection with the use of this information.

This book is dedicated to my brother, Michael. I feel you next to me each step of this journey and I know I couldn't do this without you. This is our work. Thank you for being my heavenly guide and reminding me each and every day how important this work is.

CONTENTS

.

INTRODUCTION

Drinking to celebrate, drinking to relax, drinking to cope. I've struggled myself with drinking too much. Smoking cigarettes too. I've also grappled with the effects of addiction in my relationships. Was I helping or enabling? Expecting them to change or supporting them where they were? I was angry, judgmental, arrogant.

When I first began this project, I had no idea what was to come. I thought stories of recovery would be interesting and inspiring. I was on a self-discovery journey, and I wanted to know how it was for other women. I wanted to know what their lives were like. Their families? Their homes? It turns out, I really had no clue how much addiction could tear us apart.

I'm not sure what brought you to pick up this book, but I am happy you did. Maybe, like me, you will find hope and inspiration within these pages. Stories of warriors, women with incredible strength and determination. I am honored that these women knew the power of their stories and trusted me to share them.

While many of the people with addiction who I love are still in my life today, one person is not: my brother, Michael. I'll share pieces of his story with you throughout these pages, but if there is one message you take away from this book, I hope it is this: It is never too late. The circumstances are never too bad. It is never too far gone. You are loved, and you are needed. More than you will ever know. Your family, regardless of what you think, needs you. Your friends need you. Your children need you. You may not feel loved, but I promise you with every inch of my being that you are. *You are loved beyond measure.*

This isn't a book about how to get sober. I don't know you or what makes you tick. What I am going to share are some of my own personal stories, along with 12 other women's stories in the knowing that you will find something here that resonates with you. If you are reading a story and it doesn't do it for you, then by all means, move to the next. This isn't required reading. Take what works and leave the rest. You do you, boo.

Something I didn't know before this writing began was just how much these stories would transform my life. As I listened to these women recount their stories, my heart ached when they were abused, I cried in sadness in their lowest moments, and I smiled in pride when I saw who they have become.

Stories of despair turned into stories of triumph. These women are warriors.

Each story is unique and provides something new and different to consider. With this, stories may contain emotional triggers based on traumatic events or pain that could resonate with you as the reader. You may feel the need to avoid a story altogether. That is okay. Again, there is no right or wrong way to read this book. Take what works and leave (or save for a better day) what doesn't.

Each story was told to me by the women themselves and is being shared with their permission. I have worked to maintain the integrity of each story while using minimal creative license to respect the women and their stories as they are. To preserve privacy, the women are referred to by first names only, and in several cases, by an alias. Some other names and location details have also been changed.

At the end of every story, I have incorporated some reflections. These are optional, of course. However, to make the most of this book, I would encourage you to download the free *Warriors in Recovery* companion workbook at www.melaniemoberg.com/warriorsinrecovery and write down your thoughts and feelings as you progress. If journaling makes you squirm, set a timer on your phone for five minutes after each story, and just consider the questions. I promise you this is where the real breakthroughs happen: when we look inside and understand who we really are. *Give yourself this gift.*

Throughout the book, I speak about addiction and will commonly refer to only alcohol (as opposed to alcohol *and* drugs). This is for the sake of simplicity and ease of reading. I am speaking about whatever addiction you have in your life—be it alcohol, drugs, or behavior.

My wish for you is that you better understand yourself after reading this book. Even if nothing changes, if you are still drinking or using drugs, I hope you know that it can change if that is what you desire. I don't care how many bill collectors are calling you, who is after you for money, or what things you have said and done. None of it matters. If you are having a hard time believing that your current circumstances don't matter, read this because it always puts my pain, hurt, sadness, or anger in perspective. When I am having a crappy day, I ask myself if what I am worried, upset, or sad about is going to matter in five years. If not, then why stress now? We are all going to die. Oprah, with her billions of dollars, will be in exactly the same place you are at the end of your days: in the ground. Or in an urn, I guess. Regardless of what your life looks like today or tomorrow, we will all be going to the same place. The one thing that is different is how we chose to live the "middle time"—that time between birth and death. Oprah chose to become a media mogul. She is inspiring people every day and leaving a legacy in this world. What is your legacy? What kind of impact are you leaving today? What do you want to change about it? Anything?

Remember, the only person in this world we can change is ourselves. It might require that you ask for some help, and there is no shame in that. Know that certain situations will require help from other people, maybe even law enforcement. You deserve to feel safe. Please, ask for help. There is no one capable of changing your life but you. And you, my dear friend, are a warrior.

Before we begin, one last note about our words. First and foremost, we are human beings. Let's stop calling ourselves and our loved ones "addicts" and "druggies." We are all loved people that might have an issue with alcohol or drugs. I don't understand the point of calling ourselves addicts. I once heard someone say that we shouldn't call ourselves fat, but I couldn't grasp why until it was explained. Here it is: our body has muscle, and our body has fat, along with bones and all the rest of it. We wouldn't call ourselves "bones" or "muscle," so why are we calling ourselves fat? Instead, try saying something like, "I am working toward a better version of myself." Words matter. When I started catching myself saying negative things about myself and replacing them with more positive options, the love and respect I had for myself started to change. I don't define myself by one fragment of my life. You shouldn't either.

If alcohol or drugs have created a life you no longer desire, I encourage you to choose your words differently. Notice the difference:

SHAME WORDS	POWER WORDS
"I'm an addict."	"I don't drink."
"I can't control myself around alcohol."	"I choose not to drink."
"I struggle with xyz."	"I've chosen recovery."
Qualifier (referring to someone as the person in our lives with a drinking or drug problem)	Loved one
AH/AW/AS/AD (alcoholic husband, wife, son, or daughter)	Loved one

Using words like "choose," "choice," or "love" changes the entire tone of what is being said. You have the power here. Be kind to yourself and others. Use words that build you up, not tear you down. Own your power.

MENTAL HEALTH

Mental health means many things to many people. Sometimes positive, such as, "I'm taking a mental health day!" where we happily exclaim that we are taking a day off for our own well-being. Most of the time, however, mental health comes with a negative tone, such as, "That neighbor of mine is nuts. It's like he's bipolar or something," or "Jack from church is a little crazy, if you know what I mean."

While this book is about addiction, there is much to be said about mental health. Addiction, in itself, is actually a mental health disorder. The DSM-5 is the manual written by the American Psychiatric Association and used by mental health professionals for the diagnosis of mental health disorders. Substance-related disorders, such as alcohol use, caffeine, cannabis (pot or marijuana), tobacco, and six other classes of drugs, are included in the manual.

According to NIMH (National Institute for Mental Health), approximately 39% of individuals with an addiction also suffer from mental illness, a concept known as co-occurring disorders, dual diagnosis, or comorbidity. That percentage is based on 2014 numbers, and I would bet a bit of money (just a little—I'm not much of a gambler) that the percentage of individuals with comorbidity is much higher today. I'm not here to argue the numbers. We all know that when we are feeling down, the tendency is to drink, and when we feel ashamed, the tendency is to drink. Heck, even when we feel super excited, the tendency is to drink. Having a birthday? We go for a drink. How about a graduation? We have a drink. Your cousin Susie's daughter's preschool Christmas party? Hell, we might as well drink. I'm not judging. I'm right here with you, celebrating or sobbing, whichever it may be today.

That last one was a little bit of a stretch, but you get the idea. American culture has drinking embedded within every one of its moments—both the happy and the sad. I love Annie Grace's work, and in her book *This Naked Mind: Control Alcohol,* she states, "Alcohol is the only drug on earth you have to justify *not* taking." How powerful and incredibly true is that?

The idea that addiction is classified as a mental illness might surprise you. It certainly doesn't fit what we *think* a mental health disorder looks like. Why would alcohol or drug use be classified as a mental health disorder? Alcohol and drugs create a reward system in our brains, which reinforces the desire or need to drink or use drugs. So, we use some more, and we stop doing the things we could be doing like the dishes, going to work, paying the bills, etc. Our normal tasks become unmanageable because of our use. Sound familiar? We start to experience the slippery slope of addiction. We might lose our job, which causes us to have less money than we did before. So, we financially struggle. Despite all of that, we continue to use alcohol or drugs because now we are experiencing some depressive symptoms. It becomes hard to get out of bed, we start isolating ourselves by turning down invitations to book club night or skipping church, but now we also feel bad about all of that, so we drink to feel better. Sound familiar? Ever had a drink after a hard day at work? Me too. Ever had a drink to reward yourself? Me too.

For each and every one of us, drinking starts with Figure 1 below. If we continue to drink or use drugs in an abusive manner, Figure 2 might better represent our situation.

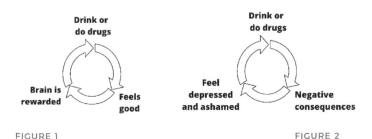

FIGURE 1   FIGURE 2

It's like a hamster on a wheel going nowhere. How does a hamster get off the wheel? He either has to stop moving his feet forward, or he has to jump off the damn wheel. Both are risky business.

Stopping asks us to consider: What happens when I stop? How do I stop? It can't be as simple as just stopping, can it? And, what happens when I jump off? How do I jump off?

Both require incredible courage. They don't require perfection or a scripted method. There is no one way to stop, and there is no one way to jump off. You, my dear friend, have choices and options. But the one thing you must decide is that you are ready to take back your life and find peace, whatever that looks like to you.

For some people, this means going to a treatment center for help. For some, it might mean finding a 12-step program, Smart Recovery meeting, or other forms of social support. It might mean that you start to see a counselor or therapist. It might mean you learn to love yourself again. I can't tell you how to heal, but I can provide some insight into the options that are available.

If you are reading this book and you are struggling—either with your own addiction or a loved one's addiction—perhaps you will find hope and inspiration in these pages. Maybe you'll read about something that worked for someone else and try it on. Maybe you'll hear a story that reminds you of your own and know that you are not alone.

My brother decided to jump off his hamster wheel. He did it by killing himself while he was drunk and high on meth. I wish that wasn't the path he took. I wish he had tried jumping off another way. Maybe he could've found sobriety and a whole new way of life, a new sense of peace. Maybe he could've been a father to his son and a husband to his girlfriend. I will never know, and that is a feeling I never wish on anyone.

I will also never know the pain my brother was in. I cannot simplify his struggles into finding a treatment program and getting on with his merry little life. Just like I can't do that for you. Only you know your struggles. Only you know your pain. But I do know that in between the depression and anxiety, there are moments of light that if you can take some action—any action—in a positive way, it can set you free. I know this in the deepest parts of my soul. I wish that my brother could go back in time and find one of those light moments and move forward. If only.

Suicide and suicidal ideations, when someone is thinking about or planning suicide, are real threats. In the United States, alcohol is involved in 20–40% of all suicides, and contemplation of suicide is up to 120 times more likely among adults with alcohol problems (Pompili et al., 2010). In fact, within the brave stories in this book, you will find that at least half of them either attempted suicide or thought in depth about planning their own death. It sounds impossible, but it's the hard reality for more than 50% of the contributions to this book. This isn't some made-up statistic. Unfortunately, suicide is happening all around us. One thing that was clear in each of the stories where suicide is mentioned is that the woman in the story where an attempt was made didn't want to die once she realized what was happening. Once she realized.

That's the tricky part. You can't be aware of your truth in a dark moment. It's impossible to think positively or clearly. There is no rationalizing why life matters with oneself. But in moments of light, we can make a change. We can make a step toward freedom, toward peace. To do this, though, you must take advantage of being in the light.

Right now, reading this book is a light moment. You are taking positive action by reading other people's stories and learning a bit about addiction and mental health in the process. In your journal, write down what your ultimate favorite day looks like. What are you doing? Who are you with? Where are you? What do you see? What do you smell? Close your eyes and envision it.

On my ultimate favorite day, I am with my kids, my dog, and my family at a cabin on the lake. We are enjoying each other's company, listening to some old country music (the 90s stuff like George Strait). We are fishing and barbequing, rehashing old camping stories from when I was a little kid, and enjoying the sunshine. In between, we take rides on the boat where my niece and I practice our subpar waterskiing skills. To me, that's a pretty perfect day.

But it's important to know how we would like our "normal" life to look. While I would love to be outdoors on a lake each and every day, it's simply not a possibility. So thinking of what our everyday life would look like is important too.

My normal day starts with an outdoor run where I can smell the fresh, crisp Minnesota morning air. Then, it looks like me being home to send my kids off to school and being there when they get off the bus. It involves me working on my business, catching up with friends, and making a difference in people's lives. There would be dinner in the evening with my family, and I'd get a little puppy cuddle time in there. Possibly take the dog on a short walk later that evening. There is nothing extravagant about my favorite day; it is simply about being surrounded by the people (furry and non-furry) that I love, doing the things I love to do, and smelling the smells I love to smell. That is where my joy is.

Where is yours? <u>Take a few minutes, close your eyes, and think about what your favorite day looks like.</u> Picture it in your mind. Who is there? What sorts of things are you doing? That's where your joy is. Write it down. What does your ideal normal day look like? Find pictures of it and stick them on a vision board. We all need to be reminded of what our joy is. This is yours.

When I think back to my brother and his story, I'm not sure that he could ever see clearly enough to see the light. Maybe he did see it, but I'll never know. I hope that you never wonder if it could have been different. I hope that you are brave enough to experiment and see what greatness you can create. It doesn't take a special background or a huge number in your bank account. Let's challenge ourselves to see what we can really do. I guarantee it's more than you give yourself credit for doing.

In the following stories, Madison, Sharon, and Kayla all have moments where they want to end it all. When they didn't think they could go on anymore. Each woman's story is very different, yet what makes them similar is that each woman is incredibly grateful that they didn't kill themselves. They are here to do this thing called life. It's not always easy, but this world needs us. It needs Madison, Sharon, and Kayla. And it certainly needs you. Never ever be afraid to ask for help. Every Oprah needs a Gayle.

MADISON

"You have the capacity to change. You just have to find it."

Madison's story is remarkable. She is blessed to have found recovery at a young age. However, recovery didn't come easily for Madison, and it almost didn't come at all.

Have you seen the movie *Big Hero 6*? I haven't, but with a little help from Google, I was able to learn a bit about it. In the movie, Tadashi Hamada builds Baymax, a robot that is designed to care. Baymax turns out to be a hero and best friend to Hiro. It's no surprise then that Madison's saving grace is her dog, appropriately named Baymax. I'll tell you about Baymax in a little bit.

Madison grew up in a small town in rural northern Minnesota. It was the type of place with little for kids to do. You can imagine that with little to do, trouble came easily. Madison was active in dance but found herself unlike other girls her age. She felt different. The boys were easier to identify with, and Madison often found herself hanging around the boys outside of dance, especially the older ones. Madison began drinking around 12 years old. The drinking progressed, and she found herself getting into trouble. Some might call getting busted by your parents for drinking in high school a rite of passage. For Madison, it was a sign of a much bigger issue.

Madison dated a guy who was a few years older than her in high school. The relationship was abusive—verbally, emotionally, and physically. It wasn't just Madison receiving the abuse; she was doling it out too. Madison's drinking continued, and dating an older guy ensured that she would have easy access to her drug of choice. After high school graduation, Madison moved to the Twin Cities for college. She moved into a house with her older sister, a mother figure in her life. She did well in college, but when the relationship with her boyfriend ended, and she found herself drinking alone at home, she became a self-described loner. The school she attended was not a known party school, so although Madison had some fun and was able to sneak out every now and then, it never got too out of control.

Until one night, Madison's life took a dramatic shift. She was the designated driver (DD) for a night out with friends at a concert. However, Madison started drinking before they even left for the night. Hours later, she found herself staring at the white ceiling above her hospital bed, bruises covering her body, and nine stitches in her forehead. No one knows what happened to Madison that night. Not Madison and not her friends. When she awoke at the hospital, she saw her dad and brother there, who had been out of town hunting that weekend.

In hearing Madison tell this story, the tone of her voice and her presence made it known that she was disappointed that she had taken her family away from something they loved.

It was a heartbreaking moment, but it wasn't enough for Madison to change. Shortly after that hospital visit, Madison found herself blacking out again. She had started talking to her ex-boyfriend on and off. She was manipulative, and she would hang out with his friends just to irritate him. This particular night, Madison only remembers waking up to her ex yelling at her. She believes they slept together that night, but she'll never know. She blacked out and couldn't remember a thing. It was scary that she didn't know. She felt horrible and ashamed. Her drinking spiraled.

Her parents' concern began to grow after Madison took a trip with her mom to Ireland. As they were getting ready to head to the airport to leave Ireland and come back home, Madison ended up missing her flight. She was drunk and lost her passport. Her parents were starting to realize the significance of Madison's drinking.

This "not knowing what happened" thing was starting to bother Madison. Why couldn't she hold her alcohol? Why couldn't she stop drinking? Why was her life spiraling out of control? Shame was building, and it had only just begun. The drinking had become a daily occurrence.

After college graduation, Madison started a job at her grandparents' veterinary clinic. The benefits of working for your grandparents were plenty in this case: she could come and go as she pleased and get out of work easily. So, getting out of work was exactly what she did. On those days, she would stay in her studio apartment, alone, drinking with her dog, Baymax.

Madison had a disorder now known as excoriation disorder—a variety of obsessive-compulsive disorder (OCD) that involved picking her own skin. Madison had experienced this disorder from a young age, but it was never really diagnosed until she was about 21 years old. Part of Madison's loneliness stemmed from this disorder. She had been known as "the girl that picks her skin," and it alienated her. The picking was becoming more serious. She was bleeding and getting infections and even went into septic shock once, an infection that can kill you by causing organ failure and low blood pressure. Hospital visits were common for the disorder, and so she decided to deal with the OCD, hoping that it might solve her drinking problem as well. She went into residential treatment for it.

After a month of treatment, Madison was kicked out because she met a boy. After that, she attended an outpatient clinic (a clinic where you go to for classes and therapy but sleep in your own bed at night). While attending that clinic, she was staying alone in a hotel. The treatment was effective; her skin picking behavior decreased. However, her drinking increased because she had lost her only coping mechanism. She would attend the OCD outpatient during the day, then come home and drink a box of wine at night. It was a constant rotation of treatment, drinking, treatment, drinking.

After a month of outpatient treatment, Madison went back to work for her grandparents again. Nothing had changed. She still came and went as she pleased. She still called in when she didn't want to work. One day, Madison attended a convention for veterinarians with her grandpa. This would be the day when Madison's grandparents began to understand the graveness of Madison's drinking.

Before the convention, Madison got drunk. While there, she fell in front of everyone. She lost her phone and somehow wandered off from the convention center. Eventually, her family found her walking around downtown Minneapolis by herself. Thankfully, they got her safely back home to her studio apartment.

The shame kept building.

Madison locked herself in her apartment for four days with Baymax. She was drinking one to two liters of vodka each day on the weekends and beer during the week. The embarrassment was overwhelming, but Madison was able to block it out. She literally locked herself away in her apartment from the rest of the world. She didn't even have a phone because she had lost it.

Madison's parents finally gained access to her apartment and found her passed out. They took her by ambulance to a local hospital where her blood alcohol content (BAC) was measured at .38. Madison couldn't believe her BAC was that high. It must have been a mistake.

She was in denial.

From the hospital, Madison was put in a psychiatric ward. It was a sterile environment with brick walls and a bed. Nothing more. And this scared Madison. She wanted to go home, but her parents wouldn't come get her. She was stuck.

Madison lied to the doctor about her drinking, but he saw right through her. The doctor recommended an outpatient program for her drinking. It didn't faze Madison much at all. She drank through the program until she decided to quit the program and move in with her grandparents. It seemed like a good idea. After all, she wouldn't dare drink in her grandparents' house.

This, of course, was a lie. It was a lie she told herself. Madison disappeared for days at a time. Sometimes she wouldn't come home. Other times, she would hide in her room, drinking away her shame and loneliness.

Toward the end of June 2016, Baymax lay on the shore of a boat launch. Next to Baymax was Madison. This dog was loyal. This dog was a hero. You see, this day, some people found Madison lying next to Baymax at the boat launch. She was passed out.

This was a pivot point for Madison. Baymax was her best friend. He helped her see the reality of her situation. As she puts it, "If I was going to choose alcohol over the one thing I cared about most in my life, something was wrong."

Madison was taken to the hospital where they placed her in the ICU, sadly an all-too-familiar place by now. With a BAC of .39, detox could cause Madison to have medical complications as her body was so physically dependent on the alcohol, so after one night of monitoring in intensive care, she was put on a 72-hour hold at detox and allowed to sober up at a facility. On July 1st, Madison called her sister from detox. It was her sister's birthday, and her sister's only birthday wish was that Madison was sober. Madison was able to grant that wish. She may have been in a miserable state, but she was indeed sober. And better yet, she wanted help.

Getting into treatment was a two- to three-week process. That time gave Madison some time to reconsider the idea of treatment. And that's exactly what she did.

She tried to stay sober, but couldn't. One night, she took off with her dad's truck, drunk. When her dad found out, he was crying. She had never seen her dad cry. It was horrible. The shame that Madison knew so well had found her again.

The next night, Madison planned to end it all. She drank as usual, except this time she took all the Ambien (a prescription medication that helps with sleep) that she could find. At some point, she called a friend who she had met in detox and told him what she had done; that she had messed up. What Madison said next is such a telling point for anyone considering ending their life: "I knew right after that I wanted to live."

She wanted to live.

This friend didn't even know where Madison lived, but he was able to get help. Madison's parents awoke with the ambulance at their home. Madison was passed out lying in bed with her beloved Baymax.

Once again, the ICU became Madison's home for a few days. Her blood pressure was unstable because of the pills she had taken. After the ICU, she was transferred to a Fargo psych ward for seven days. It was another horrible experience for Madison. It reminded her of the raptor cages in *Jurassic Park*. Because Madison wasn't yet stable, she couldn't get into a treatment center.

After her release, she went straight back to drinking.

On July 24th, 2016, Madison entered treatment. It wasn't planned. In fact, she was tricked into going. The friend who she had called that night earlier in July told Madison there was a party he wanted her to attend. He picked her up for the "party" and said, "Don't hate me," as they pulled up to the treatment center. Since the night he had gotten her call, he had been secretly talking with Madison's parents. Despite Madison dragging her feet throughout treatment, she learned so much in the 30 days of treatment. She finally understood why she could not physically stop drinking. In the beginning, Madison confessed that she was in treatment to make her family happy. But at some point in treatment, that changed, and she wanted sobriety for herself. After residential care, she completed a 30-day outpatient program before moving to an intensive outpatient program (IOP) for six months.

Today, Madison lives alone with Baymax in an apartment and plans to move in with her boyfriend soon. She has worked on mending the relationships with her family and Baymax. She and her grandma even got tattoos together! Madison was oblivious to the fact that her parents knew how manipulative she was while she was using. She now acknowledges how sick her whole family had become because of the addiction.

In treatment, she realized that she had been depressed since she was about 14 years old. The hopelessness became an issue in July 2016 when her drinking was at an all-time catastrophic level. With this knowledge, Madison has learned to appreciate integrative care—addiction treatment, mental health treatment, and medical treatment—all in one spot. She has learned to have a plan for stressful situations and continues to work on managing loneliness.

Self-care and having a sleep routine is also a big part of Madison's life in recovery. She is active in the 12-step community, attending a home group, speaking and sharing her story, and doing service work. She is also attending graduate school to become an addiction counselor, hoping to work in the prison system one day.

After despising where she grew up as a child, Madison now loves it and appreciates it for what she couldn't see before. She fishes, knits, camps, hikes, and takes Baymax to the dog park.

Since leaving treatment, sobriety has been her first priority. Madison's dad once said, "I knew there was an old Maddie in you."

Which brings us to Madison's one thing: "You have the capacity to change. You just have to find it."

Reflections

1. Madison started to realize she had a problem when she was consistently blacking out. Can you think of a situation in your life that is telling you something needs to change? What needs to change?

2. There was a lot of shame in Madison's story. The shame she felt seemed to tell her that a change was needed. Have you felt shame? If so, how were you able to overcome that feeling?

3. Madison was using drinking to cope with her skin picking disorder. What are you trying to cope with that may be an underlying reason for your drinking? Is it feelings of depression, anxiety, or worry? Something else?

4. Baymax was Madison's best friend, and he was with her through it all. Mostly, though, Madison could tell Baymax anything without him judging her. Who is in your life that is like Baymax? It could be a dog, a friend, God, or even a journal. How can you honor that relationship?

5. As a Warrior in Recovery, Madison developed a strong routine in her sobriety: 12-step meetings, a sleep routine, and outdoor activity. What is your self-care routine? What would you like it to be?

Download the Warriors in Recovery companion workbook along with other bonuses and resources to help you on your journey by visiting www.melaniemoberg.com /warriorsinrecovery

SHARON
"There's hope."

Sharon got all of her things in order. She had figured out how to make sure—legally—that her kids would go to her sister and even went as far as to have the documents notarized, so when someone would find her body, they would know where she wanted her kids to be. Sharon wasn't close to her sister, but she admired her. She was a kind and loving person, the type of person you would want to raise your children if you couldn't. Sharon didn't want her parents to raise her kids. She knew what her childhood had been, and she didn't wish that on them.

Growing up, Sharon's dad was in the military. His parents had immigrated from Poland, and he was a devout Catholic. Her mother was an Irish Catholic from Colorado and had grown up with incredible wealth. Her family had the kind of money that allowed them to have a nanny, a driver, and a housekeeper. When Sharon's grandparents found out that their daughter wanted to marry a Polish man, she was disowned. Sharon's grandparents on her mother's side had a rough time. Her grandfather drank quite a bit and was abusive toward her grandmother, who eventually killed herself. No one really knows how much her mother's upbringing played into her life, but it was clear to Sharon that it made an impact.

At a young age, Sharon felt that she had to look a certain way, act a certain way, dress perfect, sound perfect. Since very young, she felt constantly judged and unloved by her mother, who never said "I love you" to her children—Sharon and her two sisters. There was no affection. There were no hugs or kisses. It was so bad that Sharon actually developed a bleeding ulcer at 13 years old. She felt like she was in the way; that she wasn't wanted or needed. Her dad constantly traveled because of his job, so he was gone all of the time. Without much of a parent at home, Sharon was lonely throughout her childhood, and that loneliness spilled into her life as an adult.

So, there she sat on the living room couch. She couldn't get to that sweet spot, the one that she describes as "when you've had just enough cocaine and alcohol that you could pass out," and she couldn't fall asleep. It was 2:00 AM, and she didn't feel like she was high or drunk. What she did feel was this horrific, indescribable loneliness. As she sat on that couch, she found herself suddenly looking out the window. She put her hands up in the air, spread out her arms, opening them to the heavens and called out, "Oh my God, what do I do now? Help me." Sharon had bought a gun and had her plan in place. Her sister would get the kids, and she could finally be done. But instead, this night, she went back upstairs and finally fell asleep. The next morning, Sharon woke thinking about Alcoholics Anonymous (AA). She went online and found a meeting.

Because Sharon's dad had been in the military throughout the time she was growing up, her family had moved every few years. Just when Sharon started feeling comfortable in her surroundings, it would be time to move. Oftentimes, right in the middle of the school year. Most of her childhood was spent in England and Germany, where she attended an American school on base, all led by the military. There was a wide range of kids there—from sixth grade to seniors in high school—and it was small, so everyone knew each other. In most places, drinking was allowed if you could see over the bar. So, lots of kids would drink until they passed out for no reason other than to get drunk. It didn't feel like home. In fact, no place ever felt like home. To make matters worse, Sharon was a shy child. She was short, overweight, and had crooked teeth. The message she received was that she was weird, different, and that nobody wanted to hear what she had to say.

That weirdness followed her all the way to Colorado where her family moved when she was 17 years old. There, Sharon met a man. It was the first man ever to show interest in her, and she took to him right away. He was five years older than her. Being naive and young, she moved out of her parents' house to live with him. He was dealing marijuana and other drugs, and drank quite a bit himself; it was just the beginning of a long and hard relationship.

They married, and Sharon worked at a brokerage firm. She had two children with him, a son and a daughter. Her husband's use turned to an addiction. He would pressure her to drink with him, and when she did, he was fine. But when she didn't, he became abusive.

At the time, it was somewhat shameful to be in an abusive relationship. Sharon couldn't share what was happening with other people. No one was waiting with open arms to hold her tight and tell her that everything would be okay. Even though they were married for 15 years, she was alone once again.

But she was strong. She filed for divorce and kicked him out of the house. Over a few years, her husband contested the divorce. She began drinking. It was a stressful time, and his abuse worsened. Even though he was out of the house, he was stalking her. The police were no help, telling her that she was emotional and lying about it. Her drinking escalated. He would show up at daycare and grocery stores where Sharon was shopping. He wouldn't talk to her, just show up and watch her. On two separate occasions, he came into the house and tried to kill her by suffocating her with a pillow. She couldn't talk to her parents because they were upset that she had married him. They had no idea what he had been doing to her because there was no way she was going to tell them about her struggles. She was petrified, absolutely petrified.

Drinking was her escape. She would wake up in the morning, get the kids ready for school or daycare, and go into work. She would come home, feed them, and put them to bed. Then she would get drunk. It was a release that allowed her to let go for a bit until the next morning when it would start all over again.

It wasn't interfering with her work, but it was definitely becoming her routine. Sharon added some drugs into her nightly routine too. After three years, her divorce became final. She didn't have many friends and felt worthless. She had been told for many years how worthless she was, and after some time, she started to believe it. Add in her drinking, and she felt incredible shame too. Sharon suffered from PTSD (post-traumatic stress disorder) from the two times her husband had tried to kill her. At the same time, she felt proud. She was managing all of this while caring for the two kids on her own. Her ex-husband had taken off after the divorce, which created a ton of pressure for Sharon, who now, as an adult, felt like she needed to look perfect and present a happy family, just as she did when she was a little girl. She went to the PTA meetings and volunteered for every field trip she could make. She told her kids that she loved them multiple times a day. She wouldn't allow her kids to feel how she had felt.

So, the drinking continued. Once the kids went to bed, she could turn up the stereo and let loose for a little bit. She could feel free. She didn't have to worry after they went to bed. She didn't have to think about the reality of her situation, either.

Sharon was making great money at an investment firm. She had bought a townhome, and life was moving along. All the while, her routine continued. But, at this point, Sharon was starting to have some consequences for her alcohol and drug use. She had a few DUIs (driving under the influence charges). Thankfully, the kids weren't with her. However, now she didn't wait for the kids to go to bed. She'd start drinking once she got off work. She would drink all night and all weekend. There was no hiding it anymore or trying to look like she had it all together. She no longer cared.

Sharon started dating Tony, a guy who enjoyed cocaine. He moved into the townhouse, and her drinking got progressively worse. She was having so much fun and figured she could stop whenever she wanted, and she didn't want to. Sharon was getting written up at work for making silly mistakes. She was responsible for millions of dollars of wire transfers, and she was not at her best anymore. She had been called to the office a few times for smelling of alcohol. Her patience was wearing thin, and she was emotionally spent. She felt like a wreck. She became incredibly mean. If you weren't one of her children, you definitely wouldn't have gotten a smile from Sharon. Then, 9/11 happened.

September 11th, 2001 is a memorable day for most of us. I bet that you know exactly where you were that day. I was a college student, and the news hit as I waited for my International Business class to start. My professor walked into class and ushered us into the auditorium, where we watched live coverage of the events. So many people lost their lives that day. So many others lost their hope. For Sharon, that day marked a downward spiral. She was working for a brokerage firm that was headquartered out of the twin towers in New York. 9/11 shut down their operations in Denver, and Sharon was laid off.

At this point, Sharon had the townhouse, was driving a brand new SUV, and was incredibly arrogant. She had never considered she would lose her job. She felt secure, and even after losing her job, she assumed she could just go get another one. But no matter what she did, Sharon couldn't get a job. It wasn't much better on the home front, either. She'd been asked to leave a PTA meeting after other parents smelled alcohol. Her drinking was now an all-day affair. Neighbors knew about it—there was no hiding it with all the fighting that was happening between her and Tony. She picked up another DUI and some public intoxication charges. She had an interlock fitted on the ignition of her car that wouldn't allow her to drive anywhere without blowing a clean breath test.

Sharon thought this whole time that she could quit drinking whenever she wanted. But now she wanted to and she couldn't. It became clear that it wasn't that easy. She couldn't even look at herself in the mirror. She hated who she had become. She was feeling bad about how she was treating her children and others. She couldn't be nice to anyone, least of all herself. It was showing up in every area of her life.

And so, in those early morning hours, she asked God for help. She reached out her arms to heaven and asked God for help. He answered her that next morning when Sharon found a meeting for 9:00 AM and told Tony to look after the kids because she was heading out.

At the meeting, Sharon was so angry. She remembers many people coming up to her and trying to console her. She wouldn't have any of it. But one lady told her to keep coming back and shared some meeting times with her. Sharon went back to the same location the next morning and sat as close to the door as a person could possibly be. There was every sort of person in that meeting, probably 60 people in total. Sharon was now on day two without alcohol, and she was miserable. She physically felt as though she was dying. At the meeting, this guy named Bobby told her, "Do this thing like you did that shit out there." That stuck with Sharon, and so she did—she focused all of her energy into meetings.

Her attitude was still horrible. She was angry and unapproachable. She joked that the women were scared to death of her. But every meeting she attended, they encouraged her to keep coming back. And she did.

Every day for the first two years of sobriety, Sharon wanted to drink. Every single day. Her relationship with Tony fell apart— he wasn't interested in being sober. She watched as her SUV was repossessed and her townhome was foreclosed. She couldn't find a job. Everyone kept telling her, "Don't leave before the miracle happens." Sharon would roll her eyes and wonder what miracle would come. Everything she had was gone. She knew if she ever had a drink again that she wouldn't be able to get sober. She doesn't think she would recover if she ever did.

During this time, when everything was being pulled away from Sharon, lots of blessings came her way as well. A friend offered their condo for her and the kids to stay. She had come out of a meeting with an envelope under her car's windshield wiper with a few hundred dollars in it so she could buy her kids Christmas presents. Bags of groceries appeared. Little blessings showed up all the time. After two years of sobriety, Sharon says that the obsession to drink lifted. It was her miracle.

Sharon went back to college and got not just one degree but three of them. She found a job that she loves. She owns her own home and found a passion for motorcycles. Today, Sharon has over 15 years of sobriety. Her relationship with her son is incredibly strong, as it always has been. Her relationship with her daughter is not so easy as she is serving a sentence in a Colorado prison for some drug-related offenses.

As for Sharon's parents, Sharon has learned to accept that her mom did the best she could with what she had. Her father was supportive of her recovery, and they became very close until he passed in 2014. Sharon made amends with her older sister. Her younger sister struggles with alcohol, and Sharon has learned boundaries and acceptance with her.

From her very first meeting, Sharon felt hope within the walls of the meeting rooms. Just keep going until your miracle happens.

Which brings us to Sharon's one thing: "There's hope."

Reflections

1. Sharon had a tough relationship with her mother growing up. She didn't feel love and wasn't shown affection. Think about your childhood. What experiences from your childhood have shaped your present life?

2. Sharon had a day when she raised her arms and asked God for help. If you could ask God for help, what help would you ask of Him?

3. Courage will be needed for recovery to be possible. Sharon showed incredible courage by finding a meeting and attending without knowing anyone. How can you show courage on your road to recovery?

4. As a Warrior in Recovery, Sharon showed patience and hope while she waited for her miracle of recovery to come. How can you demonstrate patience and hope while you wait for your miracle?

Don't forget that you can download the Warriors in Recovery companion workbook along with other bonuses and resources to help you on your journey by visiting www. melaniemoberg.com/warriorsinrecovery

KAYLA
"Only I can define myself."

She couldn't move. She didn't know why, but she knew she just couldn't. She was lying in a hospital bed with no broken bones but on full life support complete with a catheter. She rested, soothed by the sound of a guitar. She didn't know the man who was playing beside her bed, but from what she could make out, he seemed to be a pastor. He played, and she listened intently.

After a few minutes, he got up and left. Kayla thought she'd never see him again, but the man returned. He sat down and shared the story of Job from the bible, just like a pastor would. Kayla listened. Job was a wealthy man, father to several children, and master to many servants. He owned thousands of sheep and camels, hundreds of oxen and donkeys. He was rich by all accounts, until he wasn't. He lost all of his animals and all of his children. But he did not turn his back on God. He remained faithful. In the end, God blessed him with twice as much as he had lost, and he lived a long and prosperous life.

Days earlier, Kayla had jumped out of a high window, hoping to end her life. She lay, almost lifeless, while this strange man soothed her pain with his music and words. After telling her the story of Job, he'd left, and she hadn't seen him since. She longed to see him before she was discharged from the hospital. As she was being pushed to the exit in a wheelchair, she begged to see him, but the nurse insisted that they didn't have pastors at the hospital. Kayla reasoned that the lady thought she was crazy. She had, after all, attempted to end her life. And right there, on the edge of life, this stranger had given her comfort. His words soothed. His presence was a gift. There weren't many people like him in Kayla's life. In fact, most men she had known had done the opposite of comforting her; they had hurt her. Not only physically, but emotionally. They had taken from her. This strange man didn't take anything from her. He gave something to her. Something unknown and not often felt by Kayla. He gave her love.

In the year following her discharge, she continued to call the hospital to investigate who this man was. After a while, she was told to stop calling. It seemed that this man was not a real person. But Kayla knew that no matter what, his message had spoken straight to her heart. He was there to tell her that she wasn't done yet. That just as Job had persevered after so much hurt and loss, so should she.

Kayla grew up with an amazing father, a black man who worked as a probation officer and wanted to instill values in his children—Kayla and her two brothers. He was a wonderful man with great values and qualities, but there was this one thing he couldn't stop doing: having affairs. Even though he tried, he struggled with staying faithful to her mother.

These affairs hurt Kayla's mother. Being a white woman in a

black community, she had felt outcast and ridiculed. Back in the 1980s, it was severely frowned upon to be in a biracial relationship and "make mixed babies." She had dealt with racism on this point; her own mother chastised her for creating a mixed family. The affairs and racism were traumatic for the entire family and led Kayla's parents to separate and eventually get divorced.

Kayla never really fit in. She wasn't black; she wasn't white. Her skin was lighter, and her hair was "good hair"—relaxed, not kinky, or difficult like African American hair can be. Her appearance was preferred to "normal" dark skin and difficult hair. She was a traitor in the eyes of others in the place where she lived. They were jealous and violent.

When Kayla rode the bus to school, she often got attacked by black people and by white people. In this bay area neighborhood of California, there was a culture that was unaccepting of biracial people, and Kayla had to face incredible hate. That's how Kayla learned to fight. Every day, violence was pushed on her. People even threw rocks at her. So she started preparing for it. She'd throw her backpack on and get ready for the hate to come her way. She'd fight and then walk into school as though it had never happened. After school, she'd fight and then go home. Kayla couldn't be black or white, but she could be a fighter. And so it was that this became her new identity.

Kayla started hanging out with gang members. She had found people who accepted her, but every time she was with them, she was pressured to go through the initiation to become a member. Becoming a member involved having sex with every guy in the gang, a process she calls being "jumped in." After all she'd been through, Kayla didn't want to give away her power in order to belong to a gang, so she started her own. It was a clique or posse that she called Mixed Pride. The gang was made up of girls who were all biracial. They would make themselves known by bullying other people, stealing at stores, fighting people that had drugs, and then stealing the drugs. Mixed Pride never carried guns, but they were fighters.

While all this was happening, at home, Kayla's dad and stepmom worked hard to instill values that would stick. They wanted her home every night to eat dinner together at the table. They did their best to give their kids a sense of normalcy. And to a certain extent, it worked; inside their house, things seemed pretty great. But outside, Kayla was incredibly afraid that someone would attack her, or worse, rape her.

Over at her mom's house, it was a different experience. There was no sense of normalcy. No family life. When Kayla was there, she had to feed herself because her mom simply couldn't care for her. The pain from her marriage breakdown and the affairs had taken the best of her, and she had started to drink. It was as if she couldn't deal with life anymore. She'd wake up and go to sleep, and it wasn't long before heavier drugs entered the home.

By this time, Kayla was 12 years old, and she had begun

drinking alcohol and smoking weed. She was running around with kids that had drugs in their homes. One of the kids' moms was a pot dealer, so they always had it. But one day, a line of cocaine on her mom's dresser called to her. She knew what to do with it. She had seen her mom do it countless times. That's how Kayla had her first taste.

That first experience was rough. Kayla was scared. She didn't like how it made her feel. She was nauseous, she felt really awake, and her heart kept racing. She didn't like not knowing what was happening with her body. But belonging was important to her. And not using would certainly cause her to lose street cred. Turning down drugs was weak. She'd tried, but the typical response she'd get was, "What the hell are you doing? Don't be a punk. We'll kick your ass." So, instead of looking weak, Kayla started using. It didn't always feel good, but every time became less scary than the last, and easier to handle. She still hated the feeling, but it didn't stop her. She soon found out that using had its benefits: it made her skinny, it allowed her to get more done in a day, and it kept her awake at night so she could steal things from people who were sleeping. She felt invincible. That was the feeling she craved, and it was worth all of it.

When she was 13 years old, she found herself in a clique of people who used drugs daily. Most of them couldn't be trusted. At one point, she was working with an older guy. Kayla would meet with him to get drugs so they could sell them. One night he had invited her to his room and offered her some water. Within 25 minutes, Kayla felt stimulated, and she knew that he had spiked her drink. She screamed and fought, making a scene. Kayla knew what he wanted; he wanted to take advantage of her, and there was no way she would allow it. She was assertive and tough. She kept fighting and screaming until he finally let her leave. He lived with his parents, and he worried that she would wake them. The experience filled her with intense anger. She hated that someone could have that kind of power over her.

It happened one more time. But this time, it was a friend's dad who spiked her drink. He had been watching her all night during a party. She had been wise enough to see that he was watching her. He gave her a spiked drink, and again, she felt the effects of the drug. She was suddenly stimulated. Her heart raced, and she was alert, wide awake. She was suspicious of her friend's dad and left early that night.

Kayla despised the loss of control from these two experiences. It was one thing to take drugs knowing what would happen, how you would feel. But these two times, she didn't have any control. She didn't want it in her body. She didn't want to feel stimulated. Coming down from those highs was unbearable.

At 15, Kayla dropped out of school. It had been hard for her. The constant fights were too much. She found a job working full-time at a restaurant. She wanted something different. She was trying to be responsible and pay the bills so that she could make some sort of life for herself. She lived with her mom, and her mom was still struggling day to day. Kayla came home one night to several of her friends just leaving her mom's house. They hadn't come to hang out with Kayla. They had come to sell her mom crack. These people weren't her friends at all. They were supplying her mom with drugs. It was business to them. When Kayla confronted her mom, she lied and denied buying drugs from Kayla's friends.

Anger began to build. Not only had men spiked her drinks on two separate occasions, but even her mom and supposed "friends" were lying to her. Everyone seemed to disappoint her. People were trying to hurt her. Only one thing was for certain: *no one could be trusted.*

Anger built into rage. The difference between anger and rage is how the emotion is handled. When a person is rageful, the anger isn't handled appropriately. Kayla was a fighter in the literal sense. She was sick of people disappointing her and using her. She was tired of the fight, but it was all she knew.

So she fought back. She decided to get her own apartment, away from her mom and the chaos in that home. The apartment didn't really have much. She couldn't afford anything even though she was working. She was drinking less and trying to be responsible. But inevitably, her past caught up with her. Her older brother found her and moved in. She didn't have the heart to stop him. He was using stimulants, drugs like cocaine and meth. Other people from her past who were using were finding her too. She couldn't seem to escape that life. She couldn't trust these people, and it frustrated her that she felt so stuck. The rage intensified.

Then one day, the car Kayla had lent her brother came back home with bullet holes in the window. Bullet holes. She had allowed him to borrow her car, and he returned it with bullet holes. He had stolen someone's drugs. Again, Kayla was disappointed that her brother was taking advantage of her and that she couldn't seem to leave behind this life she so desperately needed to put behind her. She wanted peace, but peace couldn't be found. She moved back home with her mom, but she was determined. She vowed to stay only a little while to finish school so she could get her GED. Then she would get out. Fast.

It was then, at 18 years old, that she met her husband. He was active in the military. Soon, Kayla was pregnant with their daughter. Within a short time, Kayla realized he was using. His job in the military had hidden his use. Kayla didn't think he could possibly be using while being active in the military, but one day, she walked in on him smoking meth. She hadn't seen anyone smoke it before. The rage returned. She was so frustrated that she'd missed the signs: hanging out with certain people and getting in trouble at work.

He used his charm on her and assured her that she deserved to use meth too. By now, she was a new mom, and she was tired. It would make her feel better. And so, she did. And when she did, she cried because she knew she was going to love it. This drug wasn't something she wanted in her body, yet she did want it. While she used, she thought of the hopes and dreams she had: raising her daughter and becoming a cop. It was all fading so quickly. This drug was home. She was convinced it was what she wanted.

Not only did Kayla's husband introduce her to meth, but he was also very abusive. Even during Kayla's pregnancy, he was hitting her and being incredibly manipulative. Kayla's family really enjoyed him, which fueled her rage even more. How could they like him when she knew what was happening behind closed doors? He was a likable guy to everyone outside of their relationship. It made her sick. Kayla never really loved him, but she was infatuated by him. She knew all along his values didn't align with hers.

Her husband ended up being dishonorably discharged from the military because of his drug use, so they had to leave the base and move back with Kayla's mom. Her mom started hanging out with him too, and it wasn't long before her mom and husband started using together behind Kayla's back. She found out, of course, just as she did with her friends.

Kayla began working as a nurse's assistant at a local hospital and became pregnant with her second child. Her husband was still not working after being discharged from the military, but he was dealing drugs. Her mom was helping him do it too, and Kayla felt so hurt. This was her home. This was her mom. Her husband. And they all lied and hurt Kayla in some way. Her husband was physically abusive, and her mom was so sick herself that she couldn't possibly be a good mom for Kayla. It felt hopeless and impossible. She felt the urge once again to be a different person. But it seemed that everyone and everything around her was conspiring to make her fail. She began to use again after her son was born.

When the relationship between her husband and mother grew closer, Kayla became suspicious of an affair between them. Her instincts made her question both her husband and her mom. They denied it. Kayla's mom was a pretty woman, although older, of course. When she confronted her husband, he used his manipulation to challenge what Kayla knew to be true. He would say, "Are you serious? You're beautiful. Why would I do that?" She tried to accept the idea that nothing was happening between them and began to worry that she was not thinking straight.

Kayla became pregnant with her third child. This time she was using meth at the time she found out. Once she realized that she was pregnant, she quit by some miracle. She was still working at the hospital as a nurse's assistant, so she did a little bit of research to find out if there were signs she had hurt the baby. What would happen if she continued to drink? Deep down, she knew that she couldn't continue and was somehow able to stop. However, the drinking and drug use continued all around her. Her husband and mother promised to stop, but those promises were empty, even when she threatened to leave the house with the kids.

The idea of an affair between her husband and mother kept coming back to Kayla. Was she crazy? She was sober at this point, and her mind was clear. It seemed so evident they might be having an affair. Having these thoughts was making her feel paranoid, just like a person would be if they were on meth. Kayla started asking friends about it. What did they think? Was it possible? Was she crazy? She asked her grandmother, her trusted source of strength, and her grandmother told her there was no way her mother would do that to her. Maybe she was just paranoid after all.

After her second son was born, Kayla began using again. Everyone around her was doing it. What was the point of not doing it too? She couldn't get away. She had tried. It was hopeless. Then, one day, Kayla just knew. There were no more questions about whether or not it was happening. She asked her mom again, who finally confessed that she had been sleeping with Kayla's husband. She felt betrayed and trapped. She wanted to take the kids and leave. But how could she?

On top of it all, her husband became even more angry and spiteful than before. His abuse amplified. One night while he was hitting her, the family was in the house too. Her mom and younger brother could hear what was happening, but they never tried to stop it. Kayla became even angrier with her family. She decided that she needed just to keep herself safe. She had no respect for her husband, mother, or brother anymore. They had all betrayed her.

One day, Kayla's daughter walked in during the hitting and screamed out, "Don't touch my mommy!" That was it. It was no longer about her. It was much bigger than her. She had quit using meth and got herself sober. She had thought she was protecting her children from what was going on, but it was evident that it wasn't enough. She called the cops.

So many stories were being told between Kayla, her husband, and her mother. Some of it was true and some of it not. It became really messy. The cops told Kayla if she didn't leave, if she didn't protect her kids by taking them out of this situation, then she would be neglectful and abusive as well. Child Protective Services (CPS) became involved. They agreed with the cops and threatened to take Kayla's kids if she couldn't change the situation.

But Kayla didn't feel like she could change the situation. Every time she left for her grandmother's house, her husband would show up. If it wasn't her husband, it was her mother. She didn't have any money to go anywhere else. Kayla's story was pretty unbelievable, and so she had to be careful with what she said to CPS. But, in the end, it didn't matter. CPS took the kids.

Thankfully, Kayla's grandmother was able to step up as guardian. Kayla and her grandmother had talked it over, and Kayla felt at peace knowing that someone she knew and trusted would be caring for her kids. CPS was suspicious that Kayla was using, and from the outside, it likely seemed that way. Her situation was messy—that was for certain. But it seemed that everything was working against her again. Here she was sober and trying to get her life together, but no one believed her. She wasn't allowed to see her kids, and she felt like she was being punished by CPS.

On one hand, Kayla wanted to become the mother she had always wanted to be, one that her kids could count on. She wanted to be dependable and provide a nice life for them. To do that, she would have to get away from her husband and her mom. It seemed impossible. She became angry again, and the rage would just build and build, so she started to use again, and the cycle continued. She would fight to become that mother that she wanted to be and then start using. It was as though there was this big rock to climb, and just as Kayla was ready to climb on top of it, she would slide back down. She even began to believe all of the negative things that CPS seemed to believe: that she was not a good mom; that there was something wrong with her.

But Kayla did eventually find some footing. She was working and found an apartment large enough that her kids could move in with her. She was pushing through all of the pain and trying to do the right things for her kids. Then, Kayla's husband figured out where she lived. She let him in her house, in direct violation of a protection order. She asked him to leave, but he wasn't having any of it. He was high, and he beat her up. He pushed her, he hit her, and then he left.

Kayla was scared to report it because of her CPS case. If she couldn't keep herself safe, surely CPS wouldn't be happy with this report. But despite her fear, she told the police about her concern, about her kids, and about the CPS case because she knew that it was best to report it. It gave her the best chance of eventually providing a safe environment for her kids. One of the officers that responded was a woman named Lisa. She brought Kayla to a nearby mirror, and together they looked in the mirror. She said, "You need to see what I see." When Kayla looked in the mirror, she didn't recognize herself. Lisa said, "It's time. It's time to stop this. It's time you tell the truth."

It was what Kayla needed to hear. She had to quit protecting the situation and the people who certainly weren't protecting her. Lisa knew this all too well. Lisa had been married to a police officer who was abusive. She fought it for a long time and felt similar to Kayla: that people wouldn't believe her story; that no one would believe enough to help her. Because Lisa's husband was an officer, it was especially difficult. She had to find other officers who might believe that one of their own was abusing his wife. Lisa fought through that resistance and overcame her abuser. And now, Lisa was sharing this story with Kayla. It empowered Kayla. She felt Lisa's strength, and it started to become hers.

The officers took pictures of Kayla's face, which was pretty banged up from being hit. The fact that the police were taking pictures of her face made things real for Kayla. It felt like it was enough. Enough of all of it. No longer would she allow this to happen. She knew things needed to change. Not in a small way, but in a really big way. CPS would not allow Kayla to see her husband, but she wasn't holding up her end of the deal. Kayla was not showing CPS she was ready. It was hard. This life was all that Kayla knew. But the divorce process started, and it was the beginning of a new life for her.

The path wasn't easy. Her days and nights were hard. The meth use had ended, but alcohol had begun. It was her staple. She couldn't sleep without it, nor could she start her day without it. She would get shakes if she didn't drink, she started her day with some booze in her coffee. Kayla was no longer using meth, but she was far from sober.

The drinking interfered with her life. She wasn't making the court appearances or the CPS meetings because she would be too drunk the night before. Her addiction ramped up. She felt isolated and helpless. Perhaps she wasn't the right person to be the kids' mom. Maybe this was for the best. But a small part of Kayla wouldn't stop fighting, wouldn't allow her to quit.

Although Kayla used meth for many years, it never had the hold on her that alcohol did. Alcohol was like her best friend. Alcohol was the one thing that gave her comfort; that felt right. Everything she did was to get closer to alcohol. She would drink alcohol and try to function through life. She still knew that she needed to be sober, but there was this thing, alcohol. How could she give that up? It was torture.

Kayla had enough. She was tired of the fight, the exhaustion, and the hopelessness. She jumped from the apartment building's fourth-story window, attempting to end her life. Only, it didn't end as she thought it would. She didn't die. A resident found her on the ground and called 911. She was severely hurt and bleeding internally but miraculously had no broken bones.

The memory of the man in her hospital room, singing and sharing the story of Job, stuck with her long after she left the hospital. It gave her hope for a new life, hope in starting over, just as Job had.

After the hospital stay, it became virtually impossible for Kayla to function with her alcohol use. At a meeting with a social worker, she admitted that she wasn't using drugs, but she was drinking. "I can't stop," she said. The social worker told her that if she continued, CPS would close the case, and she would never see her kids. It was the tough love approach that Kayla had to hear. She needed someone to give it to her straight, and that's what this social worker did.

She entered a residential treatment facility and made a true effort at becoming sober. Her body was so sick that she was unable to keep food down. She would throw up and shake all the time. Her body wanted alcohol, and because she wasn't giving in, it fought back. Sobriety wouldn't last.

Kayla was still incredibly angry. Her separation from her husband was getting finalized, and she felt like she deserved something good for the hell she had been through. She found the comfort she desired in the arms of men and started sleeping around. It wasn't really enjoyable for her, but she was always drunk when it would happen. She would walk up to the bar with the sole intention of drinking and finding a man to sleep with. She liked that kind of control. She had the power in these relationships. She could use these men for what she wanted— sex—and then leave them because they were of no use to her.

This, too, was a front. She began to hate herself. She started realizing that she was wasting her time. She could be spending this time with her kids, but instead, she was using it to get drunk and sleep around. Like so many other things, though, it was a vicious cycle and continued for some time. She would get drunk, have sex, then feel horrible about it. Because she felt bad, she'd drink, and that cycle would keep repeating itself.

Eventually, though, treatment stuck with her. She was in her children's lives and visiting her grandmother. She finished the residential treatment program and began to see a therapist, who was honest with Kayla and didn't sugar-coat things. She told her that because of her history of abuse with her ex and the anger and rage that she was exhibiting, it was likely that Kayla would be abusive toward her children if she didn't find a way to channel it. At first, Kayla was mad. How could this person say she would hurt her own kids? The therapist didn't even know her. But the idea that someone—a professional—thought she might scared her.

Kayla thought about how she might channel her anger and rage. She remembered her dad working at a dojo, a martial arts training facility, where he would train people to do Kenpo, a form of street fighting. Kayla thought it would be a good discipline for her body. Maybe she could control her anger by becoming a stronger version of herself. She took some classes and began to hold her head a little higher and walk differently. She became more confident.

However, after so many years of abuse, Kayla was showing symptoms of PTSD. She would worry when she walked down the street that someone would attack her or that men would hit her. This training was helping her overcome those feelings. She felt like she could fight back if she needed. It was interesting because Kayla had been such a confident girl. She was a fighter. Then, one day, the tables turned, and her husband had the upper hand. It took this training to find that fighter again. And she did.

At the dojo, Kayla found comfort in the other fighters. They became a gang of sorts, and it felt familiar to her. They were all warriors and would compete as a team. The team became close, and she started to date a teammate.

Then, one day her coach smelled alcohol coming from Kayla during a drill. Kayla didn't deny it. She shyly admitted that she had been drinking. Her coach was upset. He called her out. "What would happen to your kids? You agreed that you would be in tip-top shape, that you would take care of yourself. What is going on in your life?"

Kayla's boyfriend had been the only person in her life who hadn't seen her drunk or using. Kayla cherished that he hadn't seen her in that way and liked that about their relationship. However, Kayla had slipped back into drinking again, and now he had seen her drunk. Kayla says she has regretted it ever since. Her drinking was threatening their relationship. She told him she would get sober. And that's what she did.

Kayla worried for a short while that she wouldn't be able to stop again, but she put those thoughts to bed. She had stopped going to meetings, and she knew she needed to go back to one. She surrounded herself with others who were committed to being sober.

Kayla found her way back to sobriety and married her partner a year later. Today, they have a blended family with Kayla's three children and his two. While Kayla doesn't have custody of her two boys, she hopes that one day they can be together again. Kayla and her husband have used up every resource they have to bring the boys home, but it hasn't yet worked. Kayla signed away her rights to her grandmother, and getting custody at this point is unlikely, but she remains hopeful. At the time of publishing, her grandmother is not willing to allow Kayla another chance at caring for her boys.

When I asked Kayla for one thing she would like to share, she mentioned how concerning it was that she would be sharing her story. What would I think? Would I judge her? Her one thing is a reflection of that. It really doesn't matter what anyone thinks. This is her story. You have yours. The only opinion that matters is your own.

Which brings us to Kayla's one thing: "Only I can define myself."

Reflections

1. List the five people who you are surrounded by the most. Kayla was surrounded by people that were hurting her. Are these people hurting or helping you?

2. Kayla found an outlet in the dojo to channel her anger. What outlets can you use to cope with strong feelings (anger, sadness, etc.)?

3. The story of Job from the bible helped Kayla find hope. Find a story that gives you hope. It could be a bible story, a story from this book, or inspiration in an article. Post something from that story in a place you see every day (the refrigerator, closet door, mirror) to remind you.

4. Kayla felt betrayal from several people in her life, most notably her mother. She found a way to distance herself from her mother. How can you create space from people who have hurt you? It could be limiting visits to once per week or once per month, or simply not seeing them until you feel differently.

5. As a Warrior in Recovery, when Kayla relapsed the last time, she knew what she needed to do to become sober. It was to find a meeting. What is something that can bring you back to sobriety if you relapse?

Don't forget that you can download the Warriors in Recovery companion workbook along with other bonuses and resources to help you on your journey by visiting www.melaniemoberg.com/warriorsinrecovery

SELF-LOVE & ACCEPTANCE

In the girl's locker room sometime in middle school, a girl, who will remain nameless on paper but definitely has a name in my head, pointed and poked at my stomach and called me the "Pillsbury Doughgirl," playfully making a comment about my fluffy middle parts. This was over 25 years ago—25 years, ladies—and I still remember it. Words sure can hurt. More than that, they can stick with us and make us doubt ourselves. And these words were the start of my self-hate journey.

I bet you can think of a similar moment or a moment when you started to realize you weren't "perfect." I wish we could be adults with the minds of little kids who really know how to love themselves. Instead, we are adults with experiences like the

Pillsbury-Doughgirl-poke that reside in our heads, reminding us of just how imperfect we most certainly are.

Have you ever heard some self-help guru ask, "When you look in the mirror, what do you see?" or "If you could change one thing about yourself, what would it be?"

Only one thing? I would think, *Shit, it would be much easier if I only had to mention only one thing I liked.* That list was a much shorter list to narrow down. I'd go with my eyes, I think. No, everyone likes to poke fun at them because they are small. So small, in fact, that when I smile, it actually looks like my eyes are closed. I have my dad's side of the family to thank for that. I will likely need surgery to lift my eyelids someday. Ugh, genetics. No, I'd have to go with my legs. They are big, not thin and sexy like a supermodel's, but at least they are strong, built from hundreds, if not thousands, of running miles. Regardless of their size, when I look down at my legs on a run, I smile. It's definitely my legs.

But, seriously, when you hear those questions, is it hard for you to say anything positive? Hell, can you even stand looking at yourself in the mirror? I still struggle with my image in the mirror some days. I am no expert here. I am simply a woman who has body image issues and is slowly beginning to love my body and my personality. Most days, my personality is more of an issue for me than my body. I am loud and opinionated. I tend to say it like it is, and I don't have much of a filter. Actually, I don't have one at all. I've tried toning down my personality, being a little less yappy at times. But it feels horrible. That isn't who I am.

Who are *you*? Notice I didn't ask who you want to be. Who *are* you? What do you look like? How can you start to love all that you are—your personality, that mole on your nose, that crooked smile? *Who* are you?

Today, while I still struggle with my body and my loudness, I definitely appreciate what both things have done for me. My body has birthed two beautiful babies, run a marathon and several half-marathons, and tolerated all the junk I've put into it (alcohol, pizza, and cigarettes, anyone?). My loudness has allowed me to help pass legislation that requires Minnesota schools to have a mental health curriculum. It has allowed me to raise tens of thousands of dollars for mental health education and awareness. It has allowed me to be myself. And I love all these things that I just mentioned. I am proud of all of them. They make me who I am. And I love me. That last sentence has taken me over three and a half decades to be remotely okay to say, let alone put in print.

One thing that has helped me find my worth is practicing gratitude. While I would love to be someone who is up every morning at 5:00 AM with a morning routine, I just am not. (Don't get me wrong—I want to be this person.) I will, from time to time, do a morning routine, but I am not consistent with it. All this to tell you when you start a gratitude practice, it is helpful to find a consistent time each day to write down a few things that you are grateful for. I learned this from self-help author Rachel Hollis, and it really helped me find the good in everyday things. For example, one day, the following made my gratitude list: that cute bunny on the trail, the smell after rain, a warm shower, getting appointments made, and my pants fitting. These aren't mind-blowing things. They are everyday things that I found myself feeling grateful for. I would encourage you to list at least one thing every day about yourself that you are grateful for. It could be cute hair, fresh nails, how you stood up to someone, or how you comforted someone when they needed it. Celebrate you and show yourself how grateful you are for yourself. I am grateful for you.

One other item that Rachel Hollis taught me was to never break a promise to myself. (Sidebar: I now realize I am starting to sound like an RH fangirl in a scary kinda way. She came into my life when I needed to hear some hard stuff, and what she said resonated greatly with me.) I am not perfect with this one either, but holy game-changer. If I tell myself that I am going to run the next morning before going to bed, I make sure that I lay out my clothing and have my inhaler next to the bed. My earbuds are charged and ready to go. When my alarm goes off in the morning, I take my inhaler and hit my snooze. (Yes, this is risky business, but I need a little time for my inhaler to kick in— at least that's what I tell myself.) Then, when that alarm goes off again, and I don't feel like getting out of my warm bed, I remind myself that I don't break promises to myself, and I get up. Okay, I get up about 95% of the time. I'm not perfect. When I started keeping promises to myself, I started respecting myself. Try it. It changed my life.

Lastly, there is a hard truth that I want to share because it resonated with me in a big way. You may dislike me for a bit or for a long while after this one, so please take a deep breath and just consider it. You don't have to make any rash decisions today. Just consider it. Something Lisa from our next story taught me is this: we have what we are willing to tolerate. If there is someone or something in your life that you do not like, ask yourself if you are okay with it. Remember, only you can change your life. If someone or something is in your life, that is because you are allowing it. This isn't always easy to accept. Sometimes the people we love are the things we are tolerating. If so, we must decide if we are still willing to tolerate them. We may need to create some space so we can evaluate the situation. There is much to be said in this space for boundaries as well, but I will cover that in the Codependency chapter, and you can find more on my blog. For now, simply be aware that if you are unhappy with someone or something in your life, it is possible that you are not doing what is needed to protect your emotional and/or physical space. The questions after Lisa's chapter will help with this. I encourage you to reflect and journal on these questions.

Since this is a book about addiction, it is likewise important that we ask ourselves the tolerance question about alcohol and/ or drugs. In your journal, list all the pros and cons of drinking or using. Take a good, solid look at the pros side. My guess is these are short-term things: feeling good, taking the edge off, numbing the pain, socializing with friends, etc. Take a look at the cons side. What do you have there? Lost marriage, bad relationship with kids, siblings, parents, and money trouble, perhaps? These are all long-term things. That alcohol or drug we are using provides short-term benefits and causes long-term problems. Is that what we deserve? Is that what we want? If yes, then by all means, continue to use the way you are. I am not here to tell you to be sober. But, if there are things listed on that list that you don't want, you have the ability to change them. You can. You are strong. You are courageous. You get to decide what is in your life. If using doesn't make you happy, then be the change you wish to see. Nothing changes if nothing changes. You are loved, and you are a warrior. Please ask for help.

I am still a work in progress, and I will forever be working on loving myself. Self-love is work that never ends. Notice I didn't say that I hit my perfect weight and started to love myself. I am not doing all the things I want to be doing. I am not perfect. But I do my best to be grateful for who I am and what I have, I work hard on keeping the promises I make to myself, and I know what I am willing to tolerate. We must always know our beauty and our worth.

The next three stories you will read are from Lisa, Cindy, and Brenda. Each one of these women had to learn to love and accept themselves. One string throughout each story in this book, not just these three, is how each and every woman felt as though she didn't belong or wasn't good enough. This caused each woman to try to be someone they weren't while hiding behind alcohol and drugs. I know you'll find hope and inspiration in the pages that follow.

LISA

"Don't give up, and don't give in."

What are you willing to tolerate? That is the question I had for myself after hearing Lisa's story. So many times in life, I've found myself asking this question. Sometimes it can take a tragedy to answer it honestly. For me, it took losing my brother to suicide even to be aware that I could ask myself that kind of question, even to allow myself the space to ask it. A friend shared this question with Lisa and found herself at a turning point. When you read Lisa's story, ask yourself, "What am I willing to tolerate?"

Lisa grew up in Akron, Ohio. Everyone she knew worked in the tire industry—Goodyear, Goodrich, Firestone—you name it. Her family knew rubber. Lisa was the youngest of five girls in her family. When she was born, her family moved from a one-bedroom house (yes, you read that right, seven people in a one-bedroom house) to a suburb of Akron. Here, there were nice homes and expensive cars, but Lisa's family lived on some acreage outside of town in a home that had a coal furnace. They didn't have a washer and dryer because if they washed their clothes with the well water, it would turn them all rusty colored. So, they had to bring their clothes to the laundromat in town for washing.

None of this seemed odd until Lisa went into high school and started noticing what other kids had. On their 16th birthdays, they were getting TransAms. Lisa slowly realized that her family was poor. They didn't compare to these other families.

For Lisa's 16th birthday, her sister promised that she would give her a perm. At the last minute, her sister said she wouldn't do it—that she was going out instead. Lisa said, "But you promised. My birthday's tomorrow." Her sister responded with, "I don't care, kid" and left. So, Lisa decided that she would perm her own hair. It didn't end well. She ended up burning her hair, and it started falling out. Most of it had to be cut off, and she ended up with a David Bowie haircut—short and boylike. Her memory of this time is solidified with a picture of her blowing out candles on the cake with this crazy haircut. For her birthday, she simply wanted to have a nice perm like the other girls in school. Instead, she kept feeling like she couldn't measure up.

Around this time, Lisa found solace in a half-pint of vodka that her dad had hidden in his filing cabinet. She would take a shot and feel the burn of it run down her throat. It felt warm. She figured if one shot was good, two was better, and soon enough, she was filling up the half-pint with half water to hide the fact that someone was drinking her father's vodka. Alcohol made her feel warm and fuzzy, accepted, and good enough. At senior high church camp, she learned that she and her friends could go hide behind one of the buildings where a tractor was parked. There, they would huff gas to get high. Lisa started feeling pretty great about herself.

Lisa was hanging around the wrong kind of people and eventually began dating the son of the biggest drug-dealing family in the Greater Akron area. Experimenting with drugs was becoming a norm, and her goal was to live a hard, fast life and die by 30 years old. Her parents were older at this point because her mother was 37 years old when she'd had Lisa. Her older sisters had moved out, and she didn't want to be a burden. She felt that her parents had worked hard for so many years, and they deserved these years together. She didn't want to be supported. She wanted to do it on her own. So, with the goal of living a hard, fast life, she left home with that boyfriend for Colorado.

Her parents did not approve. Her father told her she was making a big mistake. Her mother cried. Here was their baby girl, Lisa, who had never lived on her own, leaving town with a boyfriend with a drug problem, leaving to start a new life 1700 miles away. Her mother was heartbroken and said, "You know what? You'll never make it."

That was all the ammo Lisa needed to motivate herself to do just that—make it. She was determined that she wouldn't call her parents or ask for money. She would do this on her own. With only some dishes, two pillows, and $350 cash, Lisa jumped into a van with her boyfriend and a few others and headed for Colorado. They had no plan beyond getting to a small mountain town where they knew one person. Their friend hooked them up with a couple that had a house where they could stay for the night. It was a bad area of town. When they arrived, this couple was smoking dope and drinking. Lisa and her friends joined and thought they had hit the jackpot. But by the end of the night, the couple was shooting heroin and howling at the moon. That was too much for Lisa and her friends. Drugs were one thing, but heroin was a whole new kind of thing. It freaked them out, and they knew they had to leave. So, without a plan, they hit the road again the next day.

Lisa knew they needed a place to stay, but they had no money left after paying for the gas to get out there. If they could get jobs, she knew they could get an apartment to rent. That would buy them some time to think and come up with a plan. They found a dog groomer in town that let them use the phone. (This was back in the seventies when there were no cell phones!) Lisa opened the phone book and started calling apartment complexes to see if they had some space available. The dog groomer told Lisa that the town they were in wasn't good—but there were a few others that weren't bad. When Lisa started talking to the landlords of these apartment complexes, it became clear that she did not have any way to secure an apartment. They didn't have jobs or money for a security deposit or the first month's rent. So, Lisa and her friends decided to head back to the town that was right off the exit when they arrived, because it was pretty run down and likely they could afford something over there.

They found a sign saying Off Highway Motel and pulled

over. By the looks of it, they'd be able to afford it, Lisa thought, so she walked in by herself and asked the guy at the front desk if there was a room available for a week. The guy behind the desk looked her up and down, then finally said, "Honey, this ain't that kind of hotel. It's by the hour. There are hot tubs." Then he motioned his arm like Vanna White to the display of sex toys on the wall. Lisa was mortified. She apologized not once, but twice and ran for the door. As Lisa ran out, the man said, "Hey, I think there's an apartment for rent across the street, though.". Lisa continued to run out of the hotel and jumped in the car.

They drove across the street, where there was an L-shaped complex with six small apartments. One of them had a sign outside the door that said Manager. Lisa made her boyfriend head up there with her this time. When they knocked, a hippie old man answered the door, and marijuana smoke came flowing out. "Oh, baby, we're home!" Lisa thought. The apartments were tiny: one bedroom, a shower, a sink, and a toilet with a 2x4 kitchen. It was so tiny that you had to walk through the living room to the bedroom to get to the bathroom. Somehow, Lisa convinced this guy to let them pay at the end of the month, which gave them two weeks to get the security deposit and the next month's rent. For now, they were off the streets.

By this point, they had sold their car for $50, so they could buy some food. Lisa's boyfriend had put the car in the ditch before they left, and it bent a wheel well, so the front right tire kept rubbing. Once the chords started to show, they rotated that tire to the back and so on. The car was pretty much out of tires and useless at this point. So, Lisa walked up and down the streets until she found a restaurant that would hire her. At that time, being an 18-year-old, she wasn't allowed to serve alcohol, but she finally found a place where she could work.

After a few months of working, she woke up one day, frustrated by her life. There was some guy sleeping on their couch, which they had brought in from off the street. It didn't even have cushions on it. Her boyfriend was sometimes working and sometimes not working, so Lisa told him, "I'm going to move uptown out of this crappy place, and you're not coming unless you can get a job, work consistently, and get a paycheck!" At that point, everyone else that had come to Colorado with Lisa had left. She had stayed—determined to prove her mother wrong.

Lisa found an apartment about eight blocks north that wasn't much better. She was driving a catering truck, meeting lots of people, especially men, many of them construction workers. She started experimenting with other drugs and was introduced to cocaine and learned free-basing, which is taking a powder form of a drug and smoking it. For a while, she dated an ironworker who was an alcoholic and extremely jealous. He would hit her and smack her around. After he threatened her with a knife, she left him by jumping out of the window and running down the street.

The next man she dated was a sprinkler fitter. Compared to

the guy she had just left, this guy was refreshing. Their relationship progressed quickly, and she moved in with him. Soon, though, he became Lisa's dealer. She would sell eight balls of cocaine for him at work, at first, selling it and doing a free portion, but then she started taking more and more of it for herself and having to pay him. While he was at work, Lisa would tear the house apart, trying to find hidden money so she could pay him with it. Soon enough, he gave Lisa an ultimatum that she had to go to rehab, or he was going to throw her out. She was scared at this point because she had gotten fired from her job and didn't really know what else to do. So, she conceded. She told him, "Well, okay. Call the place, and I'll go there." He called, and the treatment facility told him that she needed to make the call and that nobody could do this for her. The next day, he left for work, and she stared at the phone for what felt like hours. With no other options, she finally called. On the way to the treatment center, Lisa and her boyfriend went to the bar and had two beers. It was a 30-day program, and Lisa began working the AA steps there.

After the treatment stay, Lisa went back to living with her boyfriend. She believed that God had taken the compulsion to drink from her so he would keep her sober. She didn't work the steps in order or take them very seriously. She wasn't attending meetings either. She was just doing it on her own. Prior to leaving for treatment, Lisa had started working for Wendy's in their management training program. They allowed her some time off and short-term disability while she was at treatment. Afterward, she returned to that job, but she didn't change anything she was doing. She was still living with the sprinkler fitter who dealt and used drugs around her. She was hanging around the same people and the same situations. Lisa felt incredibly lonely and like she was no fun now that she was sober and not using drugs.

One night, she and her boyfriend headed out to a concert with a group of friends. Before they left, Lisa remembers thinking she wasn't going to have any fun because she couldn't drink. They attended a pre-party at a friend's house. Lisa's first trip to the kitchen was a soda. Her second trip was another soda, this time with a splash of rum. On the next trip, it was rum with a splash of soda. She was off and running. That addiction was right back where she left it. At the concert, Lisa offered to watch everyone's seats and drinks while they went to the bar. While they were gone, she drank every beer they'd left with her. By the time they returned to their friend's house after the concert, Lisa was ridiculously drunk. At the post-concert party, they brought out the drugs. There was a pile of cocaine on the table, and Lisa was thinking over and over about how she could get close to it. She walked by it at one point, brushed up against it, and her boyfriend called her out. He saw her take the cocaine. Lisa got defensive, and he told her that she was embarrassing him and made her go out to the car. He made her feel so ashamed. Lisa passed out in the car that night.

She'll never forget the next morning. In treatment, she had been told that if you pick back up with the drugs or the drink, then it is like you never quit. So now, she felt full of shame, guilt, and remorse. She was blown away thinking how everything she had worked for in those three months of sobriety was gone in one night. Even so, she felt grateful because she had learned so much from that experience.

The next day she called a friend who she had gone to treatment with and shared that she relapsed. Her friend encouraged her to attend an AA meeting and went with her to the first one. From there, every day she had off work, she would find a meeting. She felt accepted within those walls, but she was still with her boyfriend who was dealing and not treating her well—at one point, he was putting lines of cocaine on the bathroom vanity, then after she went to the bathroom, he would say, "Oh good job, that was a test." It was as though he wanted her to fail at sobriety despite his encouragement to attend treatment.

At a meeting one night, Lisa complained about her boyfriend's behavior. A truck driver named Denny who was there came up to her afterward and said, "Have you ever thought about it this way ... ?" He planted the seeds to change her perspective on the situation. He encouraged her just to come back tomorrow and not drink in between. That was it. Denny was a great support person for Lisa as she worked the program. He was encouraging and supportive.

One night at a meeting, she heard a man speak at a meeting. She thought he was arrogant and didn't have a great first impression of him. As much as she tried to avoid him, this man named Jim kept approaching her. One day, they had coffee. Soon, it turned into tennis matches and lunches. A great friendship developed and he encouraged her to leave her boyfriend. Lisa felt shame and guilt about living with her boyfriend and seeing Jim so often on the side, so she told him they couldn't see each other outside of meetings. No more tennis or lunch dates. No more coffees or movies. Lisa decided to give 150% of herself to her relationship with the dealing boyfriend for 90 days. If it didn't work, then she would know that she gave it her best effort, and it wasn't meant to be.

Lisa would often complain to her sponsor about her boyfriend. Lisa's sponsor would ask her, "Is it okay for today?"

And Lisa would say, "No, it's not okay. He's being unfaithful and a jerk."

Her sponsor would respond, "Yeah, but is it okay for today? Are you going home after this?"

And Lisa would respond, "Yes."

Her sponsor would say, "Okay, so it's okay with you." Lisa slowly realized that she was tolerating the behavior. It was okay with her until it was no longer okay.

In those 90 days, her boyfriend was coming home drunk, and women were calling the house. It was miserable. By now,

Lisa was a manager for Wendy's and working 70 hours every week. Each night, she would go home exhausted. One of those nights, around 11:00 PM, a woman called looking for her boyfriend. The woman on the phone said that Lisa's boyfriend had just left her house and that they had been seeing each other for six months. She told Lisa she was stupid. When her drunk boyfriend stumbled in moments later, Lisa confronted him. He said that he was going to deal with the girlfriend, whatever that meant, and went straight back to the other woman's house. Lisa was appalled by the whole situation. She grabbed everything she could, shoved it in her car, and drove away just 30 minutes after she'd taken the call.

Lisa drove straight to a hotel close to where she worked and called her sponsor. She had enough money to pay for the room for the night, but she had no idea what she was going to do the next night. While they were talking, her sponsor asked casually if she had called Jim from AA. He was a good friend of her sponsor and Lisa still saw him often at meetings. Her sponsor's question created a spark, and Lisa called Jim that night. By 1:00 AM, Jim had come to meet her in a donut shop, and they chatted all through the night over coffee and donuts.

At 4:00 AM, Lisa had to get to work. There was an inventory that morning, and she was a dedicated worker. When her district manager came into the store and asked how she was doing, Lisa—tired, emotional, and completely overwhelmed—couldn't

WARRIORS IN RECOVERY

hold it in. She burst into tears. The district manager asked Lisa what she was going to do, and Lisa said that she had no money, but she wasn't going back. Lisa knew she would need two paychecks to be able to get her own place and didn't know what to do. "Why don't you stay with me?" her manager offered. It was the start of a new life.

A year and a half of dating later, Lisa and Jim got married, and today, they've got over 27 years of marriage together. Lisa has been sober over 30 years, and when she thinks back, she recalls how her one goal was to make it to 30 years old, and now she's lived double that.

Today, Jim and Lisa operate a highly successful mudjacking business. They love to travel around the world and have been to places like Australia, Laos, Cambodia, Thailand, and Vietnam. They are making incredible memories and loving life.

Which brings us to Lisa's one thing: "Don't give up, and don't give in." Lisa said that life isn't too short; it's too long to let spiral on and on. Her life wasn't going to change if she wasn't going to change. It's an inside job, and that's the hardest part. You don't have to be perfect, and you don't even have to do it great. Just do it. Do the work.

77

Reflections

1. Lisa had some bad influences in her life and took some time before she stood up to them and left. Yet she had some kind people in her life as well. Where can you meet people who will help you grow?

2. Lisa's sponsor told her that she must be okay with her boyfriend because she was tolerating it. What are you tolerating that must be okay with you?

3. Lisa realized that she didn't have to tolerate a bad relationship. Now that you know you hold the power, how can you change one of these things? What can you do differently?

4. As a Warrior in Recovery, Lisa realized that recovery was an inside job. She didn't need to do the work perfectly; she just needed to do it. What is one way you can start your journey without perfection?

Don't forget that you can download the Warriors in Recovery companion workbook along with other bonuses and resources to help you on your journey by visiting www. melaniemoberg.com/warriorsinrecovery

CINDY
"Be true to yourself."

From a young age, Cindy felt different. Learning to push her own wants and needs down was something that would pave her path into addiction. Cindy was an only child and groomed to be the perfect daughter in every way. Her mom was one of the founding members of an international cosmetics company. As one can imagine, Cindy's mom was the epitome of what a professional woman should look like, and there was an unspoken expectation that Cindy should behave and look the same. And yet, Cindy didn't feel comfortable in dresses, and she didn't like all the fuss that came with being a girly girl; it wasn't who she was. Once, Cindy had asked for a package of tube socks with the stripes on them, and her mother refused, saying they were socks for boys. This was the first of many times that Cindy would be told no; that what she wanted was not an option. So, Cindy would push down her desires.

In school, Cindy dated boys and was involved in church. She didn't really like drinking or smoking. One time, she smoked a cigarette in middle school, but she didn't like it. She snuck a drink with a friend in high school once too but didn't like that either. Cindy was attracted to guys, but she was in love with her best friend in high school, a girl. It became clear to her then that she was attracted to both guys and girls. Mostly though, Cindy was attracted to a person's soul, not their gender. By this point in time, though, Cindy was living the words her mother told her when she wanted those tube socks: "No, they aren't for you." She couldn't and wouldn't tell her friend how she felt. So, Cindy pushed down her feelings.

Drugs weren't a focal point for Cindy. There was never a moment where things just fell apart. Instead, it happened gradually. When she was young, nitric oxide at the dentist was a fun experience; she loved the feeling that gas gave her. When she was 15, Cindy had an operation and was prescribed opioids; she loved it and finally felt comfortable in her own skin.

Cindy met her husband, Jeff, during her sophomore year of college. There was something about him—he was really cute and really smart. But he was also mysterious. She was intrigued with pulling out his thoughts and understanding him. Their marriage was challenging.

Cindy became a successful realtor, making six figures by age 29. She was making much more money than Jeff and encouraged him to start his own consulting firm. Suddenly, Jeff was making more money than Cindy and began to treat her differently. He hadn't grown up with money like Cindy had. There was emotional and verbal abuse, but Cindy thought it was "fine," and they set about building their dream house together.

Cindy yearned for a family and struggled with 10 years of infertility. Endometriosis was the culprit, and in 1997, Cindy was prescribed Ultram, a medication used to treat pain. At the time she was prescribed the medication, it was believed to be non-narcotic. However, Cindy found herself needing more and more. Her doctors told her not to worry about it, but she knew something was wrong. She would go to the dentist to get pain meds. And she would shop for doctors, a practice in which people in addiction go to different clinics in an attempt to get more medication. As a realtor, Cindy had access to people's homes. She knew all the places to look to find prescription drugs: the medicine cabinets in bathrooms, nightstands in bedrooms, and kitchen cabinets. Cindy tells me she is ashamed of this behavior, but the addicted person's brain is not a logical one. When taken captive by drugs or alcohol, a person does things that most people won't. By 2003, Cindy couldn't get out of bed without Ultram.

She checked herself into a hospital where the doctors there also said that Ultram was not a narcotic. Withdrawal was a horrible experience. Cindy stayed for a five-day detox, and the doctors really didn't understand why she was there.

The couple suffered three miscarriages. Jeff couldn't be there emotionally, and the Ultram provided Cindy with a way to cope. He didn't want to adopt either, but Cindy couldn't see her life without kids. During this time, Cindy still found herself experiencing crushes on female friends. She felt stronger connections with these women than she did with her husband.

Being Christian, though, she had grown up with the idea

that being gay was against the bible, an un-Christian-like thing to do or be. So, in the peak of her addiction, she made a deal with God: "I will push it down if you will give me a baby."

God delivered. After a third and final try at IVF, Cindy became pregnant. With triplets! She didn't use prescription meds the entire pregnancy and successfully birthed all three babies via c-section in 2004. She had a small amount of narcotics at the hospital but didn't leave with any. As you can imagine, life with triplets was crazy. She breastfed all three babies for six months, which is no small feat. All babies needed to catch up on weight, so she was feeding around the clock. "Walking zombie" didn't begin to describe the way Cindy felt.

Meanwhile, her marriage continued to crumble. The distance between Cindy and Jeff widened. Both of them were so focused on the kids that neither had anything to give each other. Cindy continued to be attracted to women and struggled with that knowing. For a time, she told herself that she needed the narcotics to keep up with the kids because they give you energy when you first take them. She was lying to herself.

They hired a nanny to help with the children, and Cindy continued to use drugs while working a little bit, but much less than normal. She felt alone. Jeff was not a great source of emotional support, and her parents didn't help either. To make matters worse, the nanny started flirting with Jeff. Even though she felt alone, she did have friends. She continued to have strong feelings towards girlfriends but did what she knew best: pushed down those feelings.

In 2009, a doctor prescribed suboxone, a medication used to treat narcotic addiction. However, Cindy found herself just as addicted to the suboxone as the painkillers themselves.

By 2010, Cindy was depressed and in bed, but Jeff was completely ignorant of her struggles. She was tired, miserable, and high. And she was done with it.

Checking herself into treatment, a 28-day program, Cindy felt like a liar. Remember, she made that deal with God that if she got pregnant, she would be okay with everything else? He had blessed her with triplets, but Cindy was still using and now feeling spiritually out of touch. She felt like she had broken her promise and still felt she couldn't be gay. Incredible shame overcame her. Cindy loved God, but she hated herself.

Treatment was hard. Withdrawing from the suboxone was even worse than getting off Vicodin. Nevertheless, Cindy completed the 28-day program. When she left treatment, her husband left for a snowmobiling trip, driving right past the treatment center without picking up his wife. Instead, her parents came for her. It was then that Cindy knew her relationship was over.

After the 28 days, Cindy went to an intensive outpatient program. She went to treatment three days a week for a few hours each day. This is where Cindy met Kate, another patient in the program. Kate was emotionally and mentally strong, and

Cindy felt a connection with her. For the first time in a long time, she felt okay spiritually. All these years, Cindy had felt alone and unaccepted. Now, it was changing.

About this time, Cindy became curious about a bible study teacher from college. Through Intervarsity Christian Fellowship (ICF), Cindy had attended weekly bible studies, but suddenly her teacher, Sharon, who normally led the group, was gone. Following a hunch, Cindy decided to track down Sharon and have a chat with her. She soon learned that Sharon had become a counselor after being fired from the bible study position for being in a relationship with a woman. Cindy felt relief. Sharon was a counselor, a Christian, and gay, and she could help Cindy better understand scripture and sexuality. Her sexual preference wasn't disobeying God. She found acceptance, but more than that, she was becoming whole again. She realized she had fallen in love with Kate, and they began a relationship.

Cindy told Jeff about Kate. She had become so good at pushing down her feelings and emotions since that day she asked her mom for tube socks that Jeff had no clue about her sexuality. When Cindy asked for a divorce, Jeff was angry. Their property would be split in half, and Cindy suspects that this is what infuriated him. In a rage, Jeff went into a back bedroom and scratched up his chest then called the police on a Friday night. The kids watched out the window as the cops cuffed Cindy and put her in the back of the cop car. Cindy was in jail all weekend for domestic assault. Messy doesn't begin to describe what happened next.

Jeff obtained a restraining order on Cindy, which made it next to impossible for her to see the children. It took time for Cindy to get a restraining order against Jeff. They worked through their attorneys to arrange a schedule that allowed both of them to see the kids. It was chaotic, but eventually, the divorce became final, and Cindy and Jeff sold their dream house.

It is often said that relapse is to be expected, and there was no exception for Cindy. She was able to work through slips with her sponsor, but struggled to find the right medication to treat her depression. In 2013, she overdosed on Coricidin, an over-the-counter cold medication. Cindy had gotten into her car in the garage, turned on the ignition, and let it run while the garage door was closed. Thankfully, she had contacted Kate while she was in the garage, and Kate called an ambulance. At the hospital, a doctor spent an extended period of time with Cindy, listening to what she had been trying to convey all along: something wasn't right. The doctor changed her depression medication to a different class, and within days, Cindy felt like herself again.

Today, Cindy's parents have not accepted her sexuality and have questioned her Christianity, but her children have been great throughout. When she told her kids about Kate, they were accepting. Her oldest said, "If you love somebody, you love somebody." Sometimes, kids just get it. They still remember those little orange (suboxone) pills that she would take. Cindy and Jeff share custody of the children and co-parent well. Cindy and Kate are together, enjoying life.

Which brings us to Cindy's one thing: "Be true to yourself." You will end up self-medicating in one way or another if you are not true to yourself. You can't run away from you.

Reflections

1. Cindy's mom was an especially important influence with regard to how Cindy was able to accept herself or not. Journal about someone in your life that influenced how you felt or continue to feel about yourself. Who is it? How do they make you feel? Why do they make you feel this way?

2. Cindy's bible study teacher was instrumental in helping her find acceptance. We all need people who can remind us of our greatness. Who in your life might be able to help you do the same?

3. As a Warrior in Recovery, Cindy found that once she could be honest with herself and others about her sexuality, she found peace. She started to accept herself. What are you hiding? What one step can you take to stop hiding?

Don't forget that you can download the Warriors in Recovery companion workbook along with other bonuses and resources to help you on your journey by visiting www. melaniemoberg.com/warriorsinrecovery

BRENDA

"Suit up, show up, and trust God."

Have you ever met someone and thought, "Wow, she has it all together"? My guess is that if I'd run into Brenda 35 years ago, that's exactly what I would've thought.

Brenda grew up on a farm with her brother and sister. Her brother was several years older than her, and their lives were very different because they were so far apart in age. She remembers hearing about her brother's drinking experiences with his friends, and she couldn't wait to drink. It sounded like so much fun.

At 13, her family lost their farm. It forced them to move out of a rural school into a school in a larger, nearby city. Brenda suddenly felt like a small fish in a big pond. She didn't know most of the kids at her new school, whereas she used to know everyone. Not only did she not know them, but she felt like she didn't fit because her family was having financial difficulties. She didn't see that with any other families; they seemed to have it all together. She struggled to find her place.

It didn't take long for Brenda to realize that she would get attention for doing things like talking back to a teacher. Certain kids, the rowdy ones, would laugh, and Brenda really liked it. She had been looking for her place, and she found it amongst the crowd of drinking and smoking teenagers. Brenda's sister wasn't behaving this way. She was super smart and did well in school.

Brenda did well but only cared about her grades because it was important to her mother, and she didn't want to get in trouble.

About the time she was entering high school, Brenda dove headfirst into drinking. On one particular night, she drank an entire pitcher of screwdrivers. She didn't even bother with a glass; she drank right out of the pitcher. She blacked out and felt so sick the next morning but couldn't wait to drink again.

Brenda learned to look for the people that drank and smoked. Any chance she got, she would drink. She'd get in trouble with her mom, but never had any real consequences for her behavior. She wasn't getting in trouble with school or the police. Drinking made Brenda feel more fun. It helped her feel confident and pretty and allowed her to be able to talk to people. She was a different person when she drank, and she liked being someone different. Brenda was ready to try anything that crossed her path. She used speed, pot, and hash in addition to the alcohol. There wasn't anything she wouldn't try.

After graduation, Brenda attended college. Her parents had set her up with a checking account, but she didn't know how to use it. She didn't know how to study for classes or how to create meals. Brenda was lost and again struggled to find her way. So, she found the kids who drank. That, she could do.

During her first semester, Brenda was put on academic probation. She worked and attended school part-time during her second semester. School was never a focus for her; it was a formality. Her priority was finding a guy, because if she could find a man to marry her, then she would be taken care of and wouldn't need to worry about how to live. Her second focus was drinking. So, with finding a man to marry and drinking as her two focuses, Brenda was off and running.

Brenda dated several men. She would rack up credit card debt, move in with a guy, pay off the card, break up with the guy, and get back out on her own. It seemed that Brenda's bar for what was acceptable got lower and lower over time. She quit jobs before getting fired. Relationships got worse. Originally, Brenda wouldn't have dared date a man who had a steady girlfriend, but eventually, her bar lowered even on that score, and she would date that guy. Then she told herself she wouldn't date a married man, but then she lowered the bar there too. Her behavior became worse and worse, and there was no controlling it.

In her early 20's, Brenda got a good, steady job. She worked in a business office and seemed to fit right in. Her coworkers drank as much as she did. Some days they would all go out for lunch, and it was common to have a drink. Sometimes they would go back to work after lunch, and sometimes they would call it a day and not bother. It was acceptable behavior where she worked. She began to use cocaine and heavier drugs because other people were doing it. One co-worker offered her crystal meth, and Brenda snorted it. She felt like everything was going to be okay when she used it. Through it all, Brenda would pull herself together so she wouldn't be late or absent from work. Her work ethic was strong, and it was important for her to keep things looking good on the outside. She kept up her physical appearance. She had a nice house, a nice car. Her family didn't have a clue about her drinking or drug use.

Brenda continued with her life, dating a man that started attending AA. Brenda would attend with him in an attempt to manipulate him. She wanted him to drink because she feared that if he became sober, he wouldn't leave his wife and stay with her. While in the rooms of AA, Brenda started hearing stories of people who had done what she was doing—drinking to fit in and drinking over fear. She was so afraid of everything. One of her fears was being alone, but her biggest fear of all was that people would find out what a fraud she was. The fear was so great that she fantasized about scenarios where she would die, and afterward, people would discover what a horrible person she was. She remembers going on a flight for work where her worry was not the plane crashing, but what people might find out about her if she didn't survive. That fear kept fueling Brenda's drinking. She couldn't possibly allow people to know and see what she was doing, but she also didn't know any other way to live. The shame was incredible, and the stuff she heard at these meetings stirred up some curiosity.

Then, the health issues began. She went to the doctor and found out she had an ulcer. Brenda wouldn't tell her doctor the truth about her drinking, but he seemed to catch on to her antics. He referred her to a counselor whom Brenda began seeing on a regular basis. She lied to the counselor, as well. She kept up her habit of making sure things looked good while holding back on the messy stuff. She didn't talk about her relationships with the cheating husbands or the extent of her drinking.

She stopped drinking then and continued to see the counselor on a regular basis while attending AA and Al-Anon (a group for friends and family of people struggling with alcohol use) meetings. As she sat in Al-Anon meetings, she found herself identifying more with the alcoholic than the family members or friends who were attending.

One day, everything changed. Brenda was at work when she realized someone had put the paper in the printer the wrong way. This discovery led to a full-fledged anxiety attack. When Brenda called her counselor for help, the counselor told her that those feelings she was feeling in that moment—the racing heart, the shortness of breath, and sheer panic—those were the feelings that Brenda had been drinking over to shut off. That night, Brenda went to AA and picked up her six-month chip; it happened to be six months to the day that she had stopped drinking. There, she realized that she needed more than AA and started seeing a chemical dependency counselor and doing a variety of counseling.

Brenda still didn't trust herself. She thought that maybe this sober thing was sort of like jazzercise. You know that feeling where you think something will be a part of your life forever; then it just fades away. But soon enough, a full year had passed since Brenda had taken a drink. She also noticed that she hadn't worried about not fitting in for quite some time. Not even during the AA meetings, like she had at the beginning. Historically, AA was a man's club, and Brenda thought someone would call her out for not belonging there, but that never happened. And eventually, Brenda did belong.

What about that married guy who she started attending AA with? Well, Brenda married him. It wasn't an easy road when they began. Brenda and her partner were both recovering alcoholics. So much of their behavior was dysfunctional based on that piece alone. Counseling helped them build a strong foundation for a healthy marriage. Brenda credits God for taking all of that messiness and creating something wonderful: a new family. She now has a step-daughter and grandchildren.

Exercise has played a large role in Brenda's life. Even when she was using, exercise was a part of her life, albeit a lesser one. She enjoys running and has even trained and run a half marathon. Brenda has back issues, but she doesn't let those things slow her down. Instead, she got a trainer to help her find exercises that work well for her body. She enjoys exercise for the positive role it can play in her physical and mental health. It is the one time that she can shut off the outside world and be present.

Spirituality is a big piece of AA. Sometimes it's such a big piece that it actually deters people from attending meetings or working the steps. In the rooms of AA, Brenda says, "Jesus sort of snuck up on me." She quickly realized that a personal relationship with Jesus had changed everything for her. In her heart and mind, Brenda knows that God is in control. There are many things in life that cannot be understood. Brenda was never able to have children, a huge heartache for her. Many friends and family members were having babies, yet Brenda couldn't. She has found acceptance in this and understands that God was protecting her from something. Brenda believes that God has a reason for everything, and she will know those reasons when she gets to heaven.

Which brings us to Brenda's one thing: "Suit up, show up, and trust God." Brenda believes that you can find healing in God. If you don't know or understand what that means, then just work on being a good person with good intentions for now. Have a tiny bit of willingness to learn about God, and things will begin happening for you. If you aren't willing, then simply pray for willingness.

Reflections

1. Brenda greatly feared that people would find out she was a terrible person. Are you drinking or using drugs to hide who you are? In what ways? Being honest with the people we love is a step toward freedom from shame.

2. For a long time, Brenda didn't feel like she belonged at the AA meetings. She continued to attend and eventually felt like she belonged. Some people promise that they will attend five meetings before they decide if they will continue to attend. What commitment will you honor for your recovery? The great thing about this is that if one doesn't work, there is always another commitment to try!

3. Brenda found a great spiritual connection in her recovery. What does your spiritual connection look like? It can be church or something different, like a form of spiritual meditation. How can you honor it?

4. A panic attack after the paper was loaded incorrectly in the printer allowed for change to happen in Brenda's life. If you were to have a moment of clarity, what would you hear in that moment?

Don't forget that you can download the Warriors in Recovery companion workbook along with other bonuses and resources to help you on your journey by visiting www. melaniemoberg.com/warriorsinrecovery

THE PAST

Trust me; I love to look forward. While I find it important to look through the windshield of my car to see where I am going, there are times when looking in the rear-view mirror is necessary. Sometimes we need peace, and sometimes we need to sit back there for a bit to heal. If you have suffered trauma, it is most likely something you should work through with a therapist or counselor so that you can find peace. Peace doesn't mean that you advocate for what happened to you, but that you accept that it happened and feel the emotions that come with it.

Sometimes when we've experienced trauma, it can affect how we perceive people's actions toward us. A trauma bond is when an abusive relationship causes such an emotional hold on us that we actually mistake abuse for love. Someone may want to leave the relationship, but instead, decide to try harder or decide they won't leave despite all the abuse.

Trauma is one reason why we should examine our past. Other things, such as growing up in a troubled household, can leave footprints of distress that are best discussed with a professional. Oftentimes, our childhoods have bits of bad parts mixed in with the good. And sometimes, there are bits of good in a larger mix of bad parts. Regardless, *most* parents are doing the best they can with what they have. This does not excuse their behavior, but it can help us understand it better. Realizing this will also help us heal from what has happened.

Let me be clear. There is no list of "these are the things you should see someone about" and "these are the things that you don't have to see someone about." Sometimes we may not even realize how things from our childhood have impacted our lives today. The truth is, if you are open to therapy, I think it can do everyone some good. A whole bunch of good actually. I highly recommend it in situations where trauma exists or in situations where you can't understand why you behave a certain way. Having a trusted person to talk to can make a huge difference. It did for me.

I had never been to therapy. It seemed like the sort of thing crazy people would do, if I'm completely honest. *Frasier* reruns circulated in my head, where I envisioned a therapist in a chair and the patient lying down on a ridiculously expensive couch, staring at the ceiling. But, alas, my time had come. It was only a few months after my brother's death. I was miserable in my marriage, and I was looking for a green light. I needed someone to tell me it was okay to leave. A friend had seen a female therapist (for some reason, that she was female was important to me) and had only great things to say about her experience. If she could do it, I felt like I could do it. So, I made the appointment and went.

It was nothing like the *Frasier* episode. First of all, my therapist had a couple tattoos (therapists are normal people too!), and she made me feel comfortable right away. She allowed me to share whatever I wanted to talk about. While most of what I said centered around my marriage, I managed to slip in, "Oh, and my brother killed himself a few months ago. So, there's that." The therapist's jaw hit the floor. Well, not quite. But I did get some rather large eyes, and it seemed to me there was much more to explore than I realized. I had a lot to learn. Not only did I learn more about my marriage, I learned how to grieve my brother properly, and manage other relationships in my life as well. I continue therapy to this day as I always come away from a session with something to consider. It has been a major reason for my personal growth, and I am forever grateful for it. All of that to say, if you are scared of therapy, take a leap of faith and try it out. I got lucky with the therapist I chose, but don't be afraid to try someone else if the first person you meet with isn't a fit. There is a great fit out there for you, I promise.

A large majority of my work involved learning how to love myself again. I'm still working on this. Heck, I think I'll always be working on this. I have a whole separate chapter on self-love because I think it is *that* important.

I've worked on my childhood, I've worked on my brother's death, I've worked on my relationship with my ex-husband, with my sister, with a boyfriend, and with my kids. I've worked on career options and bosses. I've worked on my issues with body image and confidence. You name it, my therapist has helped me work on it. I am not ashamed. In fact, I am quite proud.

I found it necessary to work on my past for a bit so I could look forward to the future with a clear head. Not everyone will need to do this, but I had trauma to revisit and emotional behaviors that were formed from my past. To change my behavior, I had to revisit all the crappy places I didn't want to go. It sort of reminds me of being a kid and your parents telling you that you have to go to the dentist. You don't really want to go, yet you know it's a pretty important thing. So, you go. That's what this is like. If you think it would be helpful, you might want to go back to those dark places. But don't stay…

Don't wallow in the past. Don't get so hung up on how Aunt Susie screwed you over that you forget to look forward. Don't forget where you are going. I was at a conference once, and one of the speakers used the phrase, "It happened to have happened." That really resonated with me. There are things in your past that suck. We all have them. It's not a competition about whose child-hood sucked the most or whose family ruined them the most. It's knowing that there is a whole world full of women out there that have had crappy things happen too. Much of it isn't fair at all. Take the time you need to heal. Be patient with yourself. But, please, don't wallow back there for too long. Ask for help. Revisit what needs revisiting and then throw your hair in a top bun, put on those shades, and look through the windshield. Let's do this thing!

A family with an alcoholic or alcoholics is another whole set of issues that people will understand only once they've seen it. It is hard to explain the tiptoeing, the lying, the hiding, and the spying. It is truly something I hope you haven't experienced, yet my guess is that if you are reading this book, you know a little about this kind of life. If you didn't grow up in a family with alcohol or drug issues, I would suggest watching some movies or reading books that depict the everyday reality that exists in these homes. Good films for doing this are *August: Osage County, A Star is Born,* and *Ben is Back.* Good books include: *Meet the Mulvaneys* and *The Glass Castle,* which was made into a movie.

Sometimes we use alcohol to cope with our family. This, my friends, is a recipe for disaster. If you are doing this, I encourage you to be honest about why. We may need to take a step away from family members for a time. We may need to give ourselves the space it takes to explore our feelings. There is also a chapter on codependency in this book because it was and is a large part of my journey. If you find yourself trying to control someone's behavior, take a peek at that chapter.

Before we move on to the stories of hope and inspiration of this section, take a few minutes to journal on your past. *When you recall your childhood, what stands out? What do you remember? What is your happiest moment as a child? Your saddest? How is your family today? Is there dysfunction?*

In the next three stories, you will learn about Freedom, Courtney, and Heidi, and their roads to recovery. Each of these stories is unique and provides a different perspective on how the past and our family can impact our lives. Again, I encourage you to reflect and take some time to journal after each one.

A GIRL NAMED FREEDOM
"We can overcome and heal through anything."

For about 30 minutes after I spoke with Freedom, my jaw was still on the ground. There are some stories that are just so unimaginable. So unfathomable. The type of stories that you only see in movies. And then there is Freedom's story. To say that I was naive before this story is an understatement. It's as though I was in this cute box knowing that addiction existed but never really understanding how ugly it could get. Then, I met Freedom.

Freedom grew up in a house of addiction. Her parents owned a business and had a nice home. On the outside, everything looked pretty good. However, once a certain person walked through the front doors, a different story emerged. Freedom's dad left when she was just a baby, and the person she considers to be her dad adopted her. During her childhood, her mom and dad used all sorts of drugs and drank daily. All of those substances—alcohol, weed, meth, pills, coke—they were all available at home. She was exposed daily to chaos and crazy behavior from the drugs that her parents brought into her life. She saw all sorts of sexual behavior before she really understood what any of it was.

At 12, Freedom's dad began trying to do sexual things to her. Her mother was so out of sorts from the alcohol and drugs that she was no help, even after Freedom tried to tell her. She remembers her dad reaching up between her legs underneath the sheets in the middle of the night and screaming to scare him off. She'd yell, "Get the fuck out of here!" It is no surprise that Freedom's story of drug use starts here.

She began drinking, but weed was her thing. Freedom actually didn't like alcohol because that's what her parents were doing. They were drunk every day, and she hated what it brought into her life. She didn't want to be like her parents or have anyone think she was like them. So, instead, she became a pothead. Psychedelics were also a favorite of Freedom's because they allowed her to escape into a new world.

By the age of 13, she had an older boyfriend with a car. She was doing cocaine and trying other drugs. She quickly found that she liked the ritual of preparing her drugs. Pills were boring as there was no ritual or preparation in the use of them. On top of the drug use, she was having sex with her boyfriend. It was a young age for much of what she was doing sexually, but it was all she knew. Freedom had seen so much from her childhood and didn't realize how inappropriate a lot of that was for a girl her age.

The bad behavior spilled into the classroom, where Freedom became disruptive and disrespectful of teachers. She didn't care about school, and it wasn't long before she was kicked out. She landed at a tech school, where she did bricklaying. This new school's population consisted of 18 boys and one other girl. She found herself getting a lot of attention from the guys at school.

One of the boys, Jason, was someone she could tell anything. Freedom had a lot in her life that most people wouldn't want to share, but she found she could tell Jason everything that was happening at home. He hated her dad for it, and Freedom was happy that finally, someone cared enough to protect her.

For about a year, Freedom, Jason, and his best friend Paul would hang out together, doing all sorts of drugs. Jason was Freedom's boyfriend for about a year until they decided to be just friends. Jason was hurt after the breakup, but the trio continued to spend time together. After some time, Freedom started dating Paul.

Once she turned 18, Freedom moved out of her parents' house as fast as she could. She made more friends outside of Jason and Paul, but all of them used drugs. She lived with a girl 13 years older than her and was introduced to a whole new variety of drugs. Psychedelics were all the rage with this group of friends: ecstasy and mushrooms. Raves and rainbow gatherings, month-long hippie camping events infested with drugs, were the mainstays.

About this time, Paul started doing heroin, which devastated Freedom because it changed his personality. Things started spiraling out of control pretty quickly. Paul became so different from the man she fell in love with. She had been really into Paul this whole time, so when he started heroin, it was hard for her to watch. Eventually, he left for rehab. While there, Paul hooked up with another girl, which drove Freedom crazy. She was driving around in her car, all hours of the night, trying to find him. Finally, she found him and ended up doing heroin with him because she was scared of losing him if she didn't. In her mind, they could stay together if they did heroin together.

That marked the beginning of Freedom's journey with heroin.

Freedom and Paul got an apartment on top of a diner. She worked at strip clubs and was dancing to make some money because she couldn't hold a job anywhere else. But it didn't last long. She didn't like stripping, and it was hard to keep working while she was on heroin. She constantly needed the drug, and when she didn't have it, she was getting sick. Some people could keep it together while they were on heroin, but not her. She was looking for it all the time. She couldn't work a full night. She could only dance a few times before she needed more. Other dancers were pretty serious about stripping and making good money. It just didn't matter as much as the heroin did to Freedom. They were kicked out of their place and moved back home for a bit.

Once back home, all the feelings that Freedom had about her childhood came rushing back. She was pissed. She hated them. She had no filter and would often tell her parents how much she couldn't stand them. Her dad hated Paul, and she hated them. This whole time is a bit blurry for Freedom, but she recalls stints in rehab and lots of arguments. While Freedom's parents drank and used drugs, their use was not as reckless as Freedom's, and they were able to function. One time, her parents sent her to rehab three hours away, and she hitchhiked back home. Another time, Freedom stole her parents' car, and they ended up calling the cops. Her parents had enough and kicked her and Paul out of the house. They landed in the Kensington neighborhood in Philadelphia.

Before speaking with Freedom, I had never heard of Kensington. If you have time, I would suggest looking it up. It was the birthplace of an Irish mob that sold meth to the area. Kensington is known for prostitution, crime, and high drug use, including some of the highest heroin use in the United States. Good people from all backgrounds found their way to Kensington. Freedom herself was one of these people. Despite their problems, Freedom's family had a nice house with a pool in their backyard and owned and operated their own HVAC business, which all looked good on the outside. So good, in fact, that you would never guess she would end up in Kensington.

Freedom and Paul lived on the streets and continued using drugs. Freedom began prostituting. It allowed her to keep using, and she didn't have to commit to working anywhere. Her efforts at saving the relationship with Paul didn't work. Within a month, it fell apart. It drove Freedom mad. She didn't know how to live without him. She couldn't fathom it. She was lost. She felt addicted to him more than anything. She found herself in a dazed high, walking around Kensington, screaming out Paul's name. He wasn't there. She knew he wasn't there, but her brain didn't register any of it. She felt so lost she started smoking crack. She needed drugs so badly. She decided to cut off her long hair (which was down to her butt) for money, and she now looked like a completely different person. She continued to search for Paul, calling his mom, trying to get hold of him. Eventually, Paul's mom told Freedom that Paul had gone to rehab, but that she wouldn't give her any of the information until Freedom was no longer using drugs.

Suddenly, Freedom had some motivation to find recovery. She put herself in rehab. After seven days, she called Paul's mom and told her she was sober, but Paul's mom said that Paul had left rehab and was on his way to Berkeley in California. It was 11:00 PM and pouring rain like a monsoon outside. Freedom had no money. She simply walked out of the treatment facility without telling anyone. She didn't even bring her clothes. She left with the clothes on her back: overalls, a tank top and a pair of flip flops.

She'd get to Berkeley by hitchhiking. That was the plan. It took three or four rides and about a week's time, but she made it to California. Once there, Freedom contacted Paul's mom to find out where he was, and she found out he had gone to San Francisco instead. It was right across the Golden Gate Bridge from Berkeley, so she got another ride and found him.

When she found him, Paul didn't recognize her because she

had chopped off all her hair. In San Francisco, there is a place called Polk Street, where guys prostitute in the gay community. This upset Freedom. Despite her own experience with prostitution, she didn't want Paul doing that. Even more, she wanted him to herself, but Paul no longer wanted her. They picked up their habit right where they had left off, but having hitchhiked across the country for Paul only to find he didn't want to be with her, Freedom was hurt and not in her right mind.

When Paul left the area, Freedom went back to prostituting for money and drugs, oftentimes getting arrested. Jail started becoming a normal part of her life through the next year and a half. Then, one man who was paying her for sex offered to bring her to Reno. He promised to buy her a bunch of drugs. He had lots of money and seemed genuinely to want to help her.

She went. He bought her the drugs, and they boarded a Greyhound bus. While on the bus, she went into the bathroom and stayed for a long time. Other passengers started getting angry, saying she was smoking crack, whereas she was incredibly wasted and shooting up heroin. People on the bus were freaking out, causing the bus driver to pull over on the side of the road in Sacramento. Freedom was scared of the police and didn't want to be arrested, so she tried to run away, but it didn't work. She was arrested and landed in a Sacramento jail. For about a year, she was in and out of jail probably five more times between the drug and prostitution charges.

Between jail stays, Freedom lived on the streets in a San Francisco neighborhood called the Tenderloin, an area full of people doing drugs, and not a great place for anyone to be. She was doing drugs and prostituting. Someone punched her teeth out. Seven different men raped her. Worse yet, she was learning to accept this sort of behavior as normal.

One night, she came across this guy walking around. She knew he wanted sex, and he knew she wanted drugs. That's what the Tenderloin neighborhood was all about. So, he brought her to his hotel room, bought her drugs, and gave her money. He seemed to have a lot of money, and given the circumstances, he was a pretty nice person. She shared a bit of her story with him, and he asked if she wanted to go home. More than anything, she wanted to go home. But home was no longer the community where her parents lived and she grew up. Home was Kensington, the place where she solicited sex for money and could use drugs anytime she wanted. This man bought her a plane ticket so she could fly back to Philadelphia and get back there.

Freedom would spend another seven or so years on the streets in Kensington, using drugs and prostituting for money. She was always in and out of jail. By her estimates, up to 25 times since she returned to Philadelphia. Sometimes it was just for two weeks, other times three or four months. She would have to detox cold turkey in the cell, shitting and throwing up all over the place. It was miserable. Any time she got out, she wouldn't report to probation. Even after a three-month sentence, the first thing she would do is catch a ride to Kensington to get high. There was no other option in her mind.

She survived several overdoses and saw her life flashing before her eyes, but she came back from death. When you are about to die, you lose control of your bowels. That happened to her more than once.

Then her last stint in jail came. It was a 13-month sentence. While Freedom had trouble recalling some details in her past, understandable as it was incredibly traumatic, this day, she remembers so clearly. Every little detail she can recall. When the cops picked her up that day, she was thankful. She didn't fight them when they put her in the car. She went willingly. She knew she needed help. She was going to die without it. About nine months into this sentence and sober, Freedom started to have a clearer mind. She started to see the reality of her situation. It was hard to think rationally with a lesser jail sentence. Her system needed to be free from drugs for it to happen. Around this time, Freedom recalls a day that she was so ashamed of herself that she couldn't even look in the non-breakable mirror in her jail cell. She had lost so many teeth. Two had been lost when they were knocked out in San Francisco and the others from other punches to the sides of her face. Once, a guy had swung his crutch into her mouth, and her two bottom teeth went right through her bottom lip. Her face was a mangled mess. When she was younger, she had cared so much about her appearance. It was important to her. But now, she couldn't even face her reflection in the mirror. She forced herself to look up into the mirror, and time stopped. She looked right into her own eyes, and it was as if she could see her soul. It was beautiful. It was a split second of knowing that she didn't want to go back to that life. She was going to ask for help, and she was going to find the right people.

After that moment, it was like everything had changed. The jail in Philadelphia was a rough place. People were really mean to each other, calling each other bitches and acting aggressively. Now when she saw these girls, she was no longer afraid of them. She loved them. She loved everybody.

After her sentence was up, she went back to her mom and dad's house for the first time in 11 years. It was the first time in over 10 years of living on the streets that she had a bed of her own. She was so thankful. Within six months, she realized that she couldn't live with her parents. They were still drinking and using pot, and her mom had pills. Freedom ended up relapsing. It wasn't a horrible relapse as far as relapses go, but it was enough for her to realize that she needed to change her environment. It had scared her just enough, and she didn't want to go back to the streets. She got herself off drugs and alcohol again and went to a recovery house, where she stayed for four or five months, and it was good.

After, she moved in with Michael, a man who she'd met

before her relapse; then her parents put a down payment on a house for her. Freedom says she isn't sure if her mom was trying to make up for such a hard past, but regardless, she accepted it. Freedom married Michael and they had a son together. She knew they weren't right for each other when she married him, but he was a blessing in her life nonetheless. Today, they are separated and working towards a divorce. Freedom credits Michael as being one of the best things that has ever happened to her.

Freedom's biggest goal is to be a great mom to her son. She is now working in a treatment facility as a counselor. She teaches yoga and mindfulness and helps people recover with art, music, and dance. She wants to help people.

Which brings us to Freedom's one thing: "No matter what we go through in life, we can overcome and heal through anything." Freedom has a profound sense of gratitude for the people in her life—including her parents, who have suffered in their own lives—and she places great importance on healing and breaking generations of pain.

Reflections

1. Freedom accepted some difficult behavior from others, like her parents and her partner. What behavior are you accepting? What are you tolerating?

2. Although Freedom's parents provided a less than ideal childhood, she doesn't harbor hard feelings towards them. Forgiving others is most often for us, not for the other person. Can you provide someone in your life with grace, thereby granting yourself some peace?

3. Freedom had a moment of clarity in her jail cell when the drugs finally left her body. She looked in the mirror and knew change was needed. How can you find your moment of clarity?

4. As a Warrior in Recovery, Freedom changed her life and became a treatment counselor. What would you do, given the opportunity?

Don't forget that you can download the Warriors in Recovery companion workbook along with other bonuses and resources to help you on your journey by visiting www. melaniemoberg.com/warriorsinrecovery

COURTNEY

"Don't be ashamed of what you've been through and where you've been."

This is a story of your neighbor next door, the good girl gone bad sort of story. Of course, behind every person is a story. This one is Courtney's.

Courtney grew up in Minnesota as an active kid. She enjoyed sports such as hockey and soccer. Like most kids participating in sports, her schedule was busy, so it didn't allow for much trouble. Courtney's family was picture perfect. There was no drama. Nothing. When I think of Courtney's family, I imagine her mom as June Cleaver from *Leave it to Beaver*. I can't imagine why I would share that with you. Clearly, I'm aging myself! The point is Courtney had a great family system: supportive parents and three amazing sisters.

The strong family dynamic in Courtney's life didn't make her immune to curiosity. In her senior year of high school, Courtney began experimenting with pot. Her use remained pretty controlled since she was so active in sports. That all changed, however, when Courtney enrolled in a New York college. Courtney had felt sports were defining her life, so despite being a great athlete, she decided to focus on school and not participate in sports during college. Her pot-smoking continued.

Courtney met a girl who would introduce her to Adderall. Adderall is a medication used to treat ADHD or ADD in children and adults. It is a stimulant, and its effects are similar to meth. Like so many drugs, people use Adderall to feel good. If use continues, it's likely they'll need to continue to use the drug just to function. Like many drugs, no one begins taking Adderall expecting to become addicted. Slippery slopes are often much faster than they appear.

The girl Courtney met told her the drug would make you want to raise your hand in class. One try and Courtney knew she loved it. She got the drug from friends. She got it from other students. Students who were actually prescribed Adderall would sell it just for the cash value. Courtney knew the symptoms of ADHD and went so far as to see a doctor who would unknowingly diagnose her with it. At first, the doctor prescribed Ritalin, another stimulant drug used to treat ADHD and narcolepsy. However, Ritalin isn't as strong and doesn't last as long as Adderall, but Courtney was smart. She went back to the doctor and explained that Ritalin wasn't working well enough, and he prescribed Adderall. It was just as she wanted it.

Like many others abusing drugs, Courtney was hanging out with a bad crowd, and she was soon fair game for any drug. You name it; she would try it. Painkillers, Xanax, ecstasy, alcohol, and acid were just a few of the drugs on her rotation. Eventually, Courtney couldn't function without Adderall. It was a necessity simply to get out of bed. It helped her overcome hangovers from alcohol. Her use landed her flat on her butt, kicked out of school.

Courtney moved back home and tried taking some continuing education classes through the University of Minnesota but struggled. Surrender was all that could be done. Courtney decided to try taking a year off from classes and worked as a landscaper.

Courtney's mom was concerned. She knew Courtney was smoking pot and had told Courtney that they just needed to figure out how to manage her pot use. When Courtney recalled the next piece of her story to me, it helped me remember just how much we are loved and just how much people look out for us. She said, "Mom, it's not pot. It's Adderall." Everything finally made sense. It made sense to Courtney, it made sense to her parents, and it made sense to her sisters. Her family banded around her to help. She wasn't alone; she had her family.

They helped Courtney find help at a local treatment center for adolescents and young adults. She completed the 30-day residential program and continued her treatment with an outpatient program. Courtney also saw a counselor who specialized in working with young adults with addiction issues.

Courtney returned to school at the U of M, where she received her undergraduate degree in psychology. She is furthering her education by pursuing a master's degree in addiction studies so that she can help others who might be facing similar struggles. She hasn't had any relapses.

Many people in recovery find support groups to be essential in their recovery, but Courtney does not attend. Instead, she found her community in CrossFit. She joined a gym and found her old self: the athletic Courtney. Being part of the CrossFit community has enabled her to make friends with like-minded individuals. She just celebrated five years of sobriety.

Courtney has been tested from time to time and says that change was hard. Moving out of state not once, but twice was hard. She recommends finding new people who can support you. Courtney credits her family as being a great source of support to her and likely the reason why she is so confident in saying, "Don't be ashamed of what you've been through and where you've been."

While Courtney's story is not overly dramatic—there is no moment where her life was at risk or where things fell terribly apart—it is meaningful in many ways. Her story illustrates a growing trend of Adderall use among young adults. Drug use, such as this, is common and is happening all around us. I wanted to share Courtney's story to bring awareness to this type of drug use. Adderall is a stimulant medication most commonly used to treat ADHD. It is also used to treat narcolepsy. The generic name for the drug is amphetamine or dextroamphetamine. Adderall's effects are similar to street drugs like cocaine and meth, yet it doesn't contain the stigma that those drugs do, mostly because it is a prescription medication and viewed as safe.

With many kids being prescribed ADHD medication, more than 3.5 million by 2011, its availability is rampant. Kids without ADHD are paying other kids with ADHD for their meds, and it is widely available on college campuses. Add that availability to a widespread acceptance of use, and Adderall use is spiraling out of control. Kids also get ADHD meds by taking them from friends or family who have been prescribed or lying to prescribers about symptoms to get the drug, just as Courtney did. Adderall is typically swallowed or snorted.

The other piece of Courtney's story that is interesting to me is the fact that her recovery was based on connection through CrossFit, a form of competitive fitness. Exercise had been an important part of Courtney's life. In fact, when Courtney decided to set exercise aside for a different experience in college, she began to struggle. We all have things in our lives that are part of our identity. Activity is a critical piece of Courtney's identity.

Another reason that fitness is interesting is that Courtney uses CrossFit as a way to connect with others. At the gym, Courtney finds a connection with others, and arguably, a connection to her innermost self. Recovery happens in various forms. For some people, support groups such as Alcoholics Anonymous and Smart Recovery are the pathways to recovery. For others, connection comes from activity, such as it did for Courtney. She was able to find something that held meaning for her and prioritize it in her life once again.

Which brings us to Courtney's one thing: "Don't be ashamed of what you've been through and where you've been."

Reflections

1. Even in supportive families, addiction happens. Courtney's mom asked her about her drug use, even though it must've been hard for her to do so. How can you open up communication in your own family?

2. New experiences can foster bad behavior. If you have a new experience planned (new job, new house, a move, etc.), how can you set yourself up for success?

3. Activity was a critical part of Courtney's identity. What is essential for you? What is so important to your being that you need to incorporate it into your normal, everyday life?

4. As a Warrior in Recovery, Courtney's one thing is: "Don't be ashamed of what you've been through and where you've been." How can you own your story?

Don't forget that you can download the Warriors in Recovery companion workbook along with other bonuses and resources to help you on your journey by visiting www.melaniemoberg.com/warriorsinrecovery

HEIDI

"Find your higher power and a community."

Heidi's story is one of perseverance. There are endless things in life that can knock you down. So many ways that you will be tested and left to your own devices. Will your devices help or harm you? Will you find the strength to overcome the obstacles that come in your way?

Heidi was no stranger to obstacles. She grew up with her mother and sister. She never knew her father, and her mother was an alcoholic. Because her mother was a single mom, Heidi and her sister were often in the bars where her mom worked. Drinking was normal. People drank all the time. They drank when they were happy, and they drank when they were sad. Special occasions or regular days. Drinking was so familiar to Heidi that she didn't think anything of it. In fact, one day, when her mom had a party at the house, Heidi had fun playing bartender just like her mom. During this party, Heidi was making screwdrivers with vodka and orange juice. The adults were letting Heidi have orange juice but weren't aware that Heidi started adding a splash of vodka and then a bit more. Before she knew it, Heidi was really drunk, and she was only 10 years old.

The next morning, the whole thing was brushed off. Heidi, her sister, and her friends went shopping the next day, and they had so much fun laughing about how drunk little Heidi had gotten the night before. But overall, it was no big deal that Heidi had gotten drunk at such a young age.

Heidi didn't drink much after that until junior high school. She was participating in sports when she started junior high, but it quickly became less important. Heidi had low self-esteem, and it was easier for her to relate to the kids who were smoking pot than the ones that were playing sports. She struggled with the fact that her father had abandoned her (she never knew him) and the general environment at home with her mother and sister. So, she found normalcy with the misfits: the potheads and partiers of junior high. She smoked pot and would black out from drinking so much. Thinking back now, Heidi realizes how dangerous it was to drink until blackout, and it isn't something she would wish for any teenage girl today. At the time, though, it was what Heidi knew.

When Heidi was 16, she met a man who was 25, and they had a serious relationship. He was into cocaine, and Heidi was along for the ride. While she experimented with many drugs, her mainstays were cocaine and alcohol. This man was physically abusive, and finally, a family member helped her leave him and suggested that Heidi join the military. She thought about what her life was like at the time: drinking, drugs, and lots of her friends were being sent to detention centers. It didn't look good for her. She knew that she didn't want that for her life. The same family member who helped her suggested she join the military.

So, Heidi enlisted with the Air Force teaching people how to shoot guns. This was at a fork in the road that would change her life in a big way and very possibly saved her from getting deeper into drugs, but not alcohol.

The military was a unique experience for her. While she enjoyed her job, the base where Heidi was stationed was in Las Vegas, Nevada. Needless to say, it was a base with a party culture. She had a fake ID and partied in Vegas all the time. She worked pretty hard during the week, but on the weekends, she would let loose. She'd party all weekend, and it became really hard to make it to work on time when Monday morning came. She first received a letter of counseling, then a letter of reprimand, and eventually an Article 15. An Article 15 allows for the commanding officer to determine guilt or innocence and administer punishment to the offender. Heidi ended up having to serve 30 days in correctional custody, which is like bootcamp all over again. While Heidi was just "late for work," it was clear that it was because of her drinking.

At one point, a boyfriend that Heidi was seeing threatened that he would tell the military about her alcohol use and have them take her gun card away if she didn't start attending counseling. It was a big deal for her because her gun card was necessary for her job. So, she conceded.

Heidi did a lot of internal work while in counseling, looking at the relationship she had with her mother and not knowing her father. It wasn't too hard for Heidi to see the fact that she was an adult child of an alcoholic, but looking at her own drinking was a bit harder. There are many things about Heidi's childhood that caused her to act in certain ways. However, throughout the years, Heidi had started having more problems pile up. She couldn't get away from them anymore.

After her four years of service in the military, Heidi went to college to study journalism. She was still drinking but always making it to work. She functioned well. She enjoyed writing poetry, drinking wine, and smoking cigarettes. She ate junk food and really did not take good care of herself. She reckons she likely reeked of alcohol when she went to class every day. One day, a friend named Cara asked if she had a drinking problem. Heidi took offense to it and brushed it off. She made very good grades and graduated.

Then, when Heidi was 26, her mother was diagnosed with Lou Gehrig's disease, or ALS, a disease that causes the involuntary loss of muscle function. Watching her mother deteriorate was incredibly hard. It started with her mother losing the ability to walk, then the ability to talk and swallow. It was devastating. Since she was still going to counseling at the time, her counselor asked about her drinking, and Heidi decided to attend an AA meeting. She recalls everyone being really nice at the meeting and giving her their phone numbers. Nonetheless, Heidi figured she didn't need them because she could do it on her own. She was educated and had counseling before—she believed she was smart enough to handle it without them. She started drinking a ton of non-alcoholic beer, which actually does have some alcohol in it, and smoked quite a bit of marijuana.

Then Heidi went on a ski trip and started drinking again. The relationship she was in blew up. She was a loving and kind girlfriend when she was sober, but when she was drinking, she was unbearable and angry, like Dr. Jeckyl and Mr. Hyde. Then she walked out of a job at an ad agency that she had gotten after graduating college. Heidi was struggling with burnout at work but didn't have the tools to ask for something different. The only skill she had was walking out.

Then, one day on the way home from her mother's care facility—she was now needing full-time care—Heidi decided to stop at the liquor store and grab a travel-size bottle of alcohol. She picked up the tiny bottle and headed for home. She finished it off, but she wanted more. At this point, Heidi had already gotten another job, but at 10:00 PM on a work night, when most people would be crawling into bed for the night, Heidi drove to the liquor store to get more. This was Heidi's moment of clarity. Alcohol really had a grip on Heidi's life. It had control. Heidi realized she was addicted.

The next day was April 25, 1997, and Heidi went to an AA meeting. She was feeling pretty shy, but she had been before, and she still thought she was smarter than everyone in the room. She was educated, and now she had done quite a bit of counseling.

Yet, the people in the room had something that Heidi wanted but didn't have: they had sobriety. Heidi was desperate, and she was scared. She knew that she had something to gain by attending those meetings. So, she continued to go.

And throughout all of this, Heidi's mother was dying. Part of the AA way is making amends with the people you have hurt in your addiction. Heidi was able to make amends to her mother and truly feel all the emotions that went along with losing a parent. At six months of sobriety, Heidi's mother passed. Heidi considered drinking but instead called her sponsor. That day, she stayed at a friend's house from one of the meetings and called all the family and friends that she needed to notify. Later, she showed up at her regular meeting, distraught, and her friends from the meeting took her to dinner. Her friends from AA were there for her, but her friends from the bar were not.

Although Heidi's childhood was far from perfect, she realizes that her mother's childhood was much worse. Her mother was like most other parents: she did the best she could with what she had. Sometimes that looks like very little, and sometimes it can be a beautiful thing. Heidi has found peace in her childhood and accepted it for what it was.

Heidi has done lots of service work in Alcoholics Anonymous, and after five years of sobriety, she moved to Monterey, CA for a job opportunity. In this new life, Heidi was a braver and more courageous version of herself. She went out there alone. Five years later, she lost the man she knew as her grandfather, and shortly after that, the woman she knew as her grandmother, Daddy Denny and Mama Jo. She had no elders left after they had passed. Her mother and "grandparents" were all she had besides her sister and niece.

Heidi lost her footing after losing her grandmother. Suddenly, all the emotions from losing her mother years previously came rushing back. While she thought she had dealt with her mother's death, it seemed there was more work to do. She fell into a deep, dark depression and lost weight. She was afraid for her own mental health. She didn't think that she would kill herself, but she wasn't strong enough to know that she wouldn't. So, for a few months, Heidi lived with a friend from AA who had a home in the mountains. It was incredibly peaceful. She took those few months and grew spiritually until she found God to be the single most important thing in her life.

Then, while at an AA convention in Monterey, 12 years into her sobriety, Heidi met her husband, Mark. A few years later, they moved back home to Montana, where they had grown up just a few blocks apart but never known each other. It is such a small, small world.

These days, Heidi is taking some nutrition classes. Before Heidi was even sober, she had a passion for nutrition and wanted to be a naturopathic doctor. Now, she is at a place in life where she is able to follow her dreams because drinking is no longer her priority. So, between school, work, and her loving relationship with Mark and their two fur doggies, Heidi feels that she is at a great place in life. She is still active in AA and maintains a strong relationship with her sister. Al-Anon has also been a part of her life since her husband is in recovery as well. She wanted to improve that relationship, and Al-Anon showed her some tools that were able to help. Heidi found herself wanting to control everyone and everything around her, but she has learned that she can't take on everyone's stuff.

Which brings us to Heidi's one thing: "Find a higher power of your own understanding that can support you through your own addiction or your family's addiction, as well as a community that can support you."

Reflections

1. When she was little, Heidi wanted nothing more than to be just like her mom. When you were little, who did you want to be like? Why?

2. Grief is a hard process. Have you lost someone close to you? Consider your own grieving process. If needed, what can you do to find additional peace?

3. Heidi moved to a new state on her own in a brave fashion. What do you want to do that scares you? What step can you take to get one step closer to taking the leap?

4. Heidi realized how much of a problem she had when she drank her travel-sized bottle of liquor and wanted to leave to get more late at night. Have you had an experience like this? Are you still having experiences like this? What would you rather be experiencing?

5. As a Warrior in Recovery and once sober, Heidi learned that she wanted to attend school to learn more about nutrition. What are some goals that you want to achieve?

Don't forget that you can download the Warriors in Recovery companion workbook along with other bonuses and resources to help you on your journey by visiting www. melaniemoberg.com/warriorsinrecovery

CODEPENDENCY

Codependency is often a byproduct of addiction and mental health issues. It can be hard for both parties in a codependent relationship to function on their own. They each become so invested in the other that the relationship itself becomes unhealthy. An addicted person will sometimes work to control and manipulate the other person. The codependent person often lacks self-worth to the point that he or she defines their value by how they are able to help others.

In my own relationships, I was codependent well before I ever knew it was a thing. I worked hard to fix all the people in my life. I would help them get jobs, bail them out with money, make excuses for them, and offer to clean up their messes. In all honesty, I wanted to help them. What I failed to realize, however, is that I was doing the exact opposite. It took many years of therapy to come to the realization that everything I was doing for these people I loved wasn't helping. I wasn't getting them any closer to healthy. What I was doing was pushing myself further and further into the dark hole of codependency.

My anxiety, which was previously non-existent except for "normal" situations like the school play or speaking in front of people, was through the roof. I lost sleep worrying about the people I loved while I lay in bed. I worried about everything. When I wasn't around to babysit the adults in my life, what was happening? What were they drinking? Using? Were they messing up their work? If they went out to lunch, did they have a drink? My personal peace depended on the answers.

Not only was my anxiety high when I was away from that person, but it skyrocketed when I got home. When I asked questions, was I getting the truth? Was there vodka in that glass? Then I got to be really naggy. "Why didn't you get xyz done?" or "What did you do all day?" There's no doubt I was a miserable person to be around, but that was because of them, right?

Not quite. My time in therapy would eventually help me realize it wasn't just them. It was very much me too. Without a doubt, I had developed insecurities and self-esteem issues from years of allowing people to treat me in certain ways. I had no realization of the word "no" and no boundaries whatsoever. In a word, I was miserable.

I started working with a therapist, which was slow but powerful work. I began to see my value and played around with saying no. It was ridiculously hard to say such a small word. Would I let people down when I said it? Would they still like me?

It makes me tear up a little when I write those questions now. As sad as it sounds, those were my thoughts. I was broken. What's more, I had no idea I was broken. When I started therapy, it was to deal with the people in my life. I wanted to fix them. What I learned was that I needed to focus on myself. I learned how to say no and how to form boundaries and communicate. I learned to accept people in my life and give myself space when I needed it. In that process, I began to love myself again, regardless of whether anyone approved.

Self-love is so important that I devoted an entire chapter to it. Be sure to revisit it when you need it. Know that learning to love yourself takes time, and it is a journey that never ends. Give yourself the gift of self-love. It is life-changing.

✶ BOUNDARIES

At first, I thought creating boundaries was selfish. I had been helping others for so long that I literally couldn't imagine not cleaning up behind other people. Learning to say no was some of the hardest work I've ever done.

Eventually, I asked myself what I really wanted. The truth is that so many of the things I wanted for myself wouldn't happen if I kept saying "yes" to what everyone else wanted from me. I needed to stop being trampled by the people I loved. I was allowing them to treat me a certain way, and I was reinforcing that behavior each and every time I agreed. If I wanted to be treated differently, I had to teach the people I loved that I would no longer agree to whatever they wanted.

This is extremely hard. There is no easy route here. No pass go and collect $200. That path does not exist. You must acknowledge that you might upset some people. They might yell and scream at you. They might insult you or call you names. They might be downright jerks. Whatever you do, don't back down. You are a damn warrior. Don't forget that. Walk away if you need to, but don't you back down. Commit to your "no" and don't accept anything less. You, my friend, deserve this. Treat yourself with respect. Honor what you said you would do. Don't break that promise to yourself. Commit to "no."

Each and every time you commit to your "no," it will get easier. You will begin to see how amazing that two-letter word feels when you are doing it for the right reasons. You will start to evaluate things from a new light: "How does this make me feel?" A more extreme example of this is from entrepreneur Derek Sivers, "If it's not a hell yes, it's a no." I love this, and it helps me with hard decisions.

ACCEPTANCE

One of my biggest "aha" moments in life came while I was in my therapist's office. I had been struggling for years with how to help someone in my life. It was a unique struggle because this person was heading down a path similar to my brother, who I lost to suicide. So much of this person's path was mirroring my brother's, and it scared the shit out of me. I tried just about everything, and nothing worked.

After months of rehashing all of this disappointment with my therapist, she looked at me and simply stated, "Can you accept this person just as they are?" I'll never forget my reaction. It was one of those "are you kidding me?" looks full of disgust. How could I stand by and watch this happen? My voice shook nervously as I said, "No, I can't." My therapist continued by telling me that this person in my life might never get better. In fact, it was likely that she wouldn't. It was the reality I needed to hear.

Once I left, I couldn't really believe she had asked me about acceptance. The mere thought of it sounded so absurd, so ridiculous. There was no way I could sit by and watch what was happening. But that question sat in the back of my mind for weeks. I thought about it when I allowed my mind to quiet and slowly began to realize that I could indeed find the peace I wanted if I could accept them. Peace. It sounded surreal.

Slowly, I started accepting this person. I didn't allow myself to get caught up in her behaviors or her attitude. I ditched any expectations I had for her. I can't begin to explain the shift that happened in my life when I did this. I slowly started pulling myself away from all the things I thought I should be doing to help and just let her be. If she was to be sober, she would need to find it on her own. I would certainly help if the right opportunity presented itself, but I wouldn't be driving the car. She would. It took me stepping back and letting her take the driver's seat to find peace.

I took some space by avoiding some events where I knew she might be. Space was necessary for my mind and heart to clear. It is really hard to provide space for healing, and if I'm being honest, I wasn't in a great place when I gave space. I was pissed. I was angry. I avoided her because I knew I would blow up with all of the "shoulds" and "coulds" that I had to share. She "should" find a job. She "should" go to meetings. She "could" leave her boyfriend. "Shoulds" and "coulds" are horrible things. If you ever find yourself "shoulding" and "coulding" someone, take some time to step back and really think about what you are saying. Are you helping, or are you judging? I spent years judging the people I loved. I thought I could do better. If you were to ask me back then, I would've told you I *knew* I could do better. How frickin' arrogant is that? Quite a bit. It's taken me a long time to forgive myself for thinking I knew better. How could I possibly know what was right for someone else?

Please note that I didn't say it took me stepping back and her getting sober to find peace. It would be really nice if she were sober. I don't think I'll ever know. But I do know that her life is hers. Mine is mine. I needed to protect myself and let her be for me to find peace. I would imagine that she did find some peace from me stepping away if I were to ask her. Give your relationship the gift of peace and let your mind rest.

In the next few stories, you are going to read about Sarah, Brooke, and Emily. In each woman's story, you will see elements of codependency play out, as they do in almost every story. Please take some time to journal your thoughts after each one and see how these women's stories resonate with you.

SARAH

"Nobody is beyond help."

Sarah is a self-described army brat. Although not a typical one. Her parents were both educators working for the US Department of Defense. In the military, there are schools on the bases where the kids of the military servicemen and women attend. Her parents worked at these American schools.

Sarah's family moved often. Born in Spain, Sarah would live around the world in Italy, Germany, Japan, Albania, and The Azores, a group of small islands off the coast of Portugal. This way of life has provided Sarah with unique experiences, both good and bad.

She was the perfect student and the perfect daughter. She was a straight-A student, captain of all the sports teams. She was on the student council and newspaper. Because Sarah's parents were so academic—her father was the principal for goodness sakes—Sarah was expected to do well. Devastation would have ensued if she had gotten any grade other than an A.

Sarah was also a very sensitive child. She found herself struggling with depression and anxiety symptoms, and like many people, didn't feel like she could share her struggles with others. So, she struggled inside while maintaining a smile on the outside. Sarah had a great family, and she was smart. In her eyes, sharing her struggles would have only shown weakness, and that was not something she was able to do. She certainly wouldn't tell her mom about them.

Drinking abroad was different than in the United States. In many countries, you could drink if you could see over the bar. So, that's what Sarah did. At 15, Sarah had her first drink in Germany. It was never hard to get alcohol there.

Life wasn't exactly easy for Sarah, but one night her depression would shift deeper into despair when she was raped by an American kid. She was drunk that night, and she felt so much guilt and shame. There was no way that she could share what had happened with anyone. The very next day, Sarah's family moved to The Azores, a strange new start. She stuffed the trauma away. The thought of telling her parents about what happened never occurred to Sarah as an option. Her depression spiraled, and PTSD followed.

Stuffing trauma away will always result in mental or even physical symptoms. Most of the time, trauma will strengthen if it is not addressed. Chronic pain, fatigue, and flashbacks are just a few ways that trauma lives on. For Sarah, the trauma worsened her depression while in high school. Since asking for help and talking about mental health just did not happen in Sarah's world, she began self-harming by burning incense sticks into her skin. Self-harming by burning or cutting is one way that some people will take emotional pain and turn it into physical pain. It is a release of sorts that allows the individual to focus their pain elsewhere. This type of pain was unknown to Sarah, and she wasn't sure what was happening.

Sarah tried doing better. She'd run faster in cross country, study harder. She loved school, but she was always unhappy. Trying harder wasn't working either.

Around this same time, Sarah's eating became disordered. She would work out, sneak food, and then avoid eating or restrict it. It was a vicious cycle that repeated itself. Growing up, Sarah's mother would ask, "Should you eat that?" or "You can pull that off because you are thin." Her mother didn't mean to affect Sarah's relationship with food, but the comments did.

Life on the military bases was hard. Often, as soon as Sarah would form friendships, she would have to move to the next base. She learned to fit in well. Every time she moved to a new base, it meant she would be attending a new school with new kids. Even the language was new in most cases. But the kids attending schools were similar. Their backgrounds were similar. The parents had the same jobs, and the kids had been to the same schools. Skin color was one of the only differences between these kids. Even so, Sarah never felt like she fit in. She felt different. Always.

Sarah's sensitivities, depression, and anxiety symptoms were a piece that set her apart. She didn't know how to talk about it with anyone, nor did she want to talk about it with anyone. Complaining to her mom or other people was not acceptable. Her mom wouldn't put up with it, and other people wouldn't because everyone was dealing with the same things: new faces, new language. There was no compassion for how hard it was to live that way.

During her high school years, drinking and partying was pretty normal. Her parents were liberal and just advised that she be responsible. So, Sarah and her friends would take taxis home. Sarah received strong messages from her parents to be a good person, treat people well, give back, and be a decent human being. Sex was okay, so long as it was done responsibly. When Sarah was 18 years old, she dated a boy fairly seriously. Her parents loved him. He was the first consensual sexual partner that Sarah had. This boyfriend helped Sarah grow into her sexuality as an adult and overcome the fear of sex after the trauma she endured. She still remembered the trauma, though, but the only thing that could make it worse would be telling someone else. So, she still kept quiet.

She graduated from high school while in The Azores and left the islands for San Antonio to attend college. Her grandmother was there, and so it was a great fit. At this point in life, Sarah's drinking was actually less than normal American kids. Because she grew up drinking, it wasn't a novelty, and she could hold her liquor well. Sarah and her boyfriend mutually decided to part ways, as Sarah knew she would want to settle down, and he wasn't interested in doing so. In college, she smoked weed a few times but never really liked it. She probably would have tried other drugs, but she wasn't offered any and didn't seek them out.

After college, she taught reading and language arts at middle school level. She continued to drink, having a few glasses of wine at night after teaching. For Sarah, this was normal as her parents would have a glass or two at night. That glass or two eventually led to three or four. It was never a problem for her. There were no consequences for drinking that much, and she felt like she deserved it. She needed it. She never hung out at the bars, and she didn't like the taste of hard alcohol. But, she did like wine, a whole lot.

Sarah met her husband, Kevin, and married at 24 years old. He was stationed in the military as a physician's assistant. He moved to a base in Fort Knox, Kentucky, and she would join him as soon as her school year ended. Her drinking slowly increased. In addition to the wine, she added some vodka. Even though she hated hard liquor, vodka was the one she hated the least.

It was when Kevin deployed to Afghanistan for a year that Sarah's drinking really escalated. Without anyone to question her or call her out, she drank. She was sad, lonely, and depressed. During this time, Sarah was teaching in Kentucky in impoverished areas. Meth was present, and many students' parents were addicted to meth. The school was failing. It inspired Sarah to get her master's degree in social work.

Although obtaining her master's degree, her drinking

continued to spiral out of control. She would drive to class but worried that her classmates could smell the alcohol. Gatorade containers proved to be a good way to disguise vodka at school. She would drink vodka during class breaks and wine at night.

Sarah knew she needed some help and started seeing a therapist. Somehow, despite a lifetime of feeling that she couldn't show weakness, she was honest with the therapist about her eating issues, which she was still going through, and was recommended for inpatient treatment. Sarah took a leave of absence from work to attend. The program helped her deal with her unresolved trauma from the sexual assault, as well as her undiagnosed depression and anxiety, and disordered eating. During that month of treatment for her eating disorder, she wasn't drinking at all. Once home, however, when Sarah's eating disorder got better, her drinking became worse.

It was a vicious cycle. Sarah would drink to numb her emotions that were now raw because she was bingeing and purging less. The drinking escalated further. By now, it wasn't uncommon for her to wet her pants and be stumbling drunk. Back home from Afghanistan, her husband said nothing of it. They avoided conflict, and so this was nothing to discuss, but it wasn't long before she couldn't hide it anymore. She was found passed out at work one day, and they allowed her to quit instead of being fired. She lied to her husband and said that she quit to focus on school.

Sarah graduated in 2013 with her master's degree. Most days, she was drinking all day, a Gatorade bottle full. She worked part-time as a social worker, supervising parental visits. She would drink a bit of wine in the morning to rid herself of the shakes that often presented themselves from the previous day's drinking. Then, she would drink while working and worry that people would smell it. Several nights each week, she wouldn't end up falling asleep but passing out instead. Over time, Sarah became a great detective. After waking, she would look for glasses, text messages, or call history to find evidence of what had happened the night before.

In 2014, Sarah and her husband moved to Minnesota. She found a social work position and found herself experiencing the same problems as before. She would drink on the job. Each day, she would drive drunk to clients' homes to do assessments. Sarah had always been skilled at putting on a front. Since she grew up with parents that were focused on image, she had the training to do this well. She felt like she was doing a good job for her clients and wanted to be sure that they didn't suffer because of her drinking. She kept it all looking fine on the outside.

Sarah's first DUI came when she passed out in her car outside of a Chinese restaurant. The cops found her, and she was taken to the hospital. It was at this point that her husband stepped in and helped her get into treatment. She completed a month-long program, but after release, she couldn't stay sober and realized she couldn't have even one sip. It became so bad that Sarah's husband would take away her keys and her wallet (so she had no money or ID). It didn't matter. Sarah would hike the 2.5 miles to the liquor store in the snow and ice to shoplift vodka. Later, she would use her passport as ID. Nothing would stop her from getting alcohol.

Sarah's second DUI happened after she totaled her car. Thankfully, it was a single-vehicle crash, and Sarah was fine. She landed herself in jail for five days. When she called her husband from jail, he began to cry. She had never heard him cry before. He repeated, "Why, Sarah? Why?" over and over again. It broke her heart. There was so much shame, guilt, and remorse for what she had done and for how she had treated her family, her sisters, and her husband. This time, she had an interlock fitted on her car, where she had to blow into a tube to verify her BAC before she could start her car. She did a second treatment, this time out of state.

The last time Sarah drank was in 2016. She was on vacation in New Mexico with family and friends, but not with her husband. She didn't drink much as she recalls, but her body sent a very strong message. Sarah wasn't feeling well, and her family called Kevin to come to New Mexico so he could fly Sarah back home. Kevin tells Sarah that she was acting drunk, and he quickly noticed that she was in acute withdrawal. As a physician's assistant, Kevin could see the signs. He took her to the ER, where she seized. The doctors sedated Sarah in a coma for 10 days. Whenever they tried to bring her out of the coma, she would seize again, and her heart wouldn't tolerate it. Eventually, Sarah was able to come out of sedation safely. After such a long time of being intubated, Sarah had a hard time talking. She was so weak that she couldn't walk and needed to use a walker for a few days. She and her husband flew back home, where Sarah entered treatment for the third time. Thankfully, she has been sober since.

Sarah doesn't believe that she has another relapse in her. She believes her brain and her body are done. She believes that if she drinks, she will likely die. She had so many problems, so many wake-up calls, and yet she says none of those seemed to be what people call "rock bottom."

Sarah is active in her continuing care. She sees a therapist regularly and takes in a few AA meetings each week. She also makes time for self-care, getting a regular massage. She is also active in the sober community, meeting regularly with other moms in recovery (Sarah had a son after treatment). She has a psychiatrist and takes medication for her anxiety and depression. Sarah grew up thinking that you shouldn't tell anyone that you are struggling. Now, she believes vulnerability is strength, and that is where we can find connection with others. I couldn't agree more.

She is happier in sobriety than she ever was drinking. Which brings us to Sarah's one thing: "It's never too late. Anybody can get help." Find what works for you. If you fall down 1,000 times, get back up 1,001.

Reflections

1. Sarah's upbringing in the military caused a strong unsettling feeling. When in your life have you felt unsettled like you couldn't relax or enjoy the moment? Why?

2. Childhood was hard for Sarah, and her environment carried high expectations. Have you been held to high standards? What sort of problems has perfectionism caused in your life?

3. Sarah went to great lengths to hide her drinking. I can only imagine how stressful it must've been. What are you hiding? How is it serving you?

4. Sarah did things while drinking that she couldn't imagine doing sober, like putting her life in danger behind the wheel and not being the kind of social worker she wanted to be. What are some things you have done while drinking or using that you couldn't imagine doing if you were sober?

5. As a Warrior in Recovery, Sarah is happier in sobriety than she ever was drinking. I can only imagine that she feels an immense sense of peace. What does peace look like to you?

Don't forget that you can download the Warriors in Recovery companion workbook along with other bonuses and resources to help you on your journey by visiting www. melaniemoberg.com/warriorsinrecovery

BROOKE

"There's support and love on the other side of addiction."

Finding something that works for you is key. Brooke is our next story. In her story, I think you will find so many things that happened in her life that make you wonder: How did she get through that without drinking? For Brooke, she found something that worked for her: a support group.

Here's the thing; life is hard. Damn hard. There is not a single person on this earth who is exempt from hurt, pain, or tragedy. How we handle those hard times is what can make us or break us. When my brother died, I wallowed for many weeks. I felt sorry for myself, and I smoked cigarettes like they weren't going to make them anymore. But I didn't stay there forever or for long. I took a few weeks and felt sorry for myself. That was okay. But I quickly decided that my brother wouldn't appreciate the wallowing. He would want me to not only live my life but live a fulfilled life. Smoking cigarettes and drinking was not fulfilling. Not at all. So, I started doing things that would make him (and myself) proud. I started speaking out about his story and finding my path in life after living without purpose for quite some time. It caused a dramatic shift in my life; I got divorced and started attending graduate school to study addiction and mental health. I'm here today, still finding what lights me up and what message I want and need to share with the world. Brooke's story is one of those messages.

Brooke was saving her money to fly to Germany. She wanted to marry the boy she had dated through high school. He was stationed in Germany with the service, and Brooke couldn't stay with him there until they were married. So, they were married quickly stateside, and once Brooke had saved enough money for the flight, she joined him.

Before she left, Brooke had seen a commercial on TV for Al-Anon. She decided to take her mother. Her father had been drinking for many years and was becoming increasingly violent. Brooke worried about her mother and her ability to manage that situation while she was in Germany. Her mother really took to the Al-Anon program. Brooke's father was drinking, he was the type of dad that used hard discipline and violent outbursts were not uncommon either. There was verbal shaming, guilting, and yelling, but it would occasionally turn into physical violence, especially with Brooke's brothers.

She had two brothers, and they were both gifted. Her older brother was incredibly smart, one of those annoying kids who barely studied and got straight-As. He was a talented musician and could even write music. In comparison, Brooke felt average. She had to work hard to get any attention. She felt like if she could do better, do more, then her dad would notice her, and he would be happier. It was a ton of weight on a young woman's shoulders, but it didn't faze her. This notion of not being enough followed her to college, where she received a scholarship on an instrument because the symphony was missing the instrument she happened to play, and they gave her the scholarship on potential. They thought *maybe* she could do it. She wasn't good enough; that was the message she kept getting.

Brooke returned from Germany pregnant with a son. By this time, her father had found recovery in AA, a blessed peacefulness for him. Things seemed to be on the right path. Then, when Brooke's son was two years old, her husband up and left. Brooke wasn't prepared to handle life without him. She was alone and felt like a failure as a mother. Not only that, but she was left with a ton of stress from her husband's poor ability to manage money. They were in debt. Over the next years, her drinking increased as a way to manage the stress.

Brooke had a new goal: find a father for her son. It didn't look good that she had a son and wasn't married. She looked like a loser. She wasn't working. It didn't even matter to Brooke if this person loved her, but they needed to love her little boy. So, Brooke started going out to bars, meeting guys, and drinking quite a bit. It was there that she was introduced to the guy who fit the bill: he was a high school teacher and worked with a friend. He loved her little boy, and his family did too. A year later, they married.

Her second husband was a heavy drinker and used pot heavily. Brooke took to it too, but she still attended Al-Anon because she felt she could make everyone happy. If she could just do more for them, she could make them happy. She wanted to fix it.

Five years after they were married, the couple had a baby boy and then three years later, another baby boy. At this point, Brooke was working but was still putting up a front. She was dressing up and playing the part of a corporate housewife. She partied with coworkers and was larger than life. Her self-esteem was non-existent, though, and her behavior showed it. In the meantime, Brooke and her husband hosted weekly parties and were having a lot of fun drinking and using drugs. She didn't think her drinking was affecting anyone. After all, she was showing up for work, grocery shopping, doing the chores. Everything was still functioning...

Until one day when Brooke hit her bottom. She realized that everything she was doing was actually affecting other people. It was the morning of a normal Saturday. They were having a party later that night, hosting lots of people, and Brooke did what she would do on any day like this. She started drinking early in the day and started smoking pot to relax. The party came and went. The next morning, Brooke woke up early to clean up. As she walked around the house collecting bottles and garbage, she walked out by the pool. They had a gated fence around their pool, but as she walked over, she caught a glimpse of her baby's diaper by the steps leading down to the water. Quickly, Brooke looked into the pool to check if her son was at the bottom. Brooke realized she didn't have it together. She wasn't being a good mom. She couldn't recall if her baby had even been outside. She had been drunk. Her husband had been drunk. Her oldest son was thirteen, and her middle son was five. Her youngest wasn't quite two-years-old yet, and she didn't know if he was lying at the bottom of the pool the morning after their party. Fortunately, he was safe in his bed.

It was the wake-up call that Brooke needed. Suddenly, in a matter of two minutes, Brooke knew she needed help. She had her last drink and drugs the night of that party. She wouldn't touch it again. That was over 36 years ago. That day, she called some friends from Al-Anon who had shared their stories of being "double winners"—people who qualify for being in both the Al-Anon and AA programs. She went to a meeting that day and got started in the program. She confessed her drinking and drug use to her Al-Anon sponsor, who introduced her to her first AA sponsor. She knew about steps from the Al-Anon program, so it was a natural process for her to enter AA.

All this time, Brooke had been pretending that she had it all together, but now she told her parents what was happening. Her dad and mother were very supportive, knowing the program from her father's addiction. Her brothers were both using heavily, though, and were a mess. While Brooke was able to keep her addictions under wraps, her brothers were musicians, and their addictions were out in the open. Her relationship with her father came full circle as he shared some advice with her. He told her that he asked God, his higher power, to remove the compulsion to drink or use every morning and every night. It was a simple prayer, but it was powerful. Brooke had seen how he was and who he had become. It had been an incredible transformation, and he had, by then, 11 years of sobriety. Brooke took his advice, and she was able to stay sober and off drugs without a traditional treatment program.

One of my favorite things about Brooke's story is hearing how she felt after and continues to feel today. She says that she was joyful. She had peace and serenity. It was an incredible feeling. When she looked into her boys' faces, at last, at the age of 34, she felt like a mom. She was enjoying her family. When I listened to Brooke tell her story, there was incredible pride in her sobriety. While hearing Brooke speak about it and even as I write this now, I too feel so much pride for her. But not everyone did. In fact, her husband was less than thrilled.

Since he wasn't supportive of her getting sober or off drugs, he definitely didn't support her taking time away from the family to attend AA meetings. Brooke found a 6:45 AM meeting to attend every day. She didn't have the support at home, but she didn't let that hold her back. She found a way to work around it. By attending an early morning meeting, Brooke's husband could be with the kids first thing, and Brooke could finish getting everyone ready for school by the time she returned and then head to work herself.

Brooke tried to get her husband to attend marriage counseling with her—or even seminars and retreats—but he didn't want any part of it. He didn't know this version of Brooke, and in all honesty, Brooke didn't know this version of Brooke. The healthier she got, the sicker he became. He used more and drank more. He became violent, hostile, and really depressed. While he was great at his job as a high school teacher, he had nothing left at the end of his day. He would come home, drink, use, and crash in the lounge chair.

Thankfully, Brooke was now sober and off drugs. She could keep up with the kids' busy school and sports schedules and tried hard to show him how different life could look, but he wanted nothing to do with it. So, after another six years of pushing, she finally surrendered and filed for divorce.

The divorce was incredibly hard. He hired a top attorney and fought for full custody. In the end, the judge settled on joint custody, which was scary to Brooke since he was still drinking and using. In this process, however, he realized that he didn't just want to be a weekend dad, he wanted to be a dad. So, he cleaned up his act and became the guy Brooke had needed him to be. At this point in her life, Brooke wasn't in love with him—she just wished he had shown up earlier.

In AA, Brooke met the person who she is still married to today, some 30 years later. She has stayed sober in some incredible times. Just a few years into sobriety, after she met her now-husband, Brooke's oldest brother stumbled into traffic in an altered state and was killed. He had been drinking and using drugs for most of his life. At the time he died, he was homeless and living on the streets. He tried programs and meetings, but he just couldn't stay off drugs and sober. The day he was fatally hit by a car was, of course, heartbreaking for Brooke, who describes him as her hero.

It broke my heart to hear Brooke's loss. There are some sibling relationships that are just hard and some that are hard but still close. I think that is how Brooke felt about her brother—she was incredibly close to him despite his struggles. That is how I felt about my brother. He was my hero too. A loss like this one never goes away. Instead, it follows you and guides your every move. I greatly admire Brooke for not suffering a relapse at this point in her sobriety.

On a positive note, her other brother did find sobriety. It didn't come easily or without hardship. In fact, it wasn't unusual for Brooke to receive calls from her brother telling her it would be the last time she heard his voice, an ominous warning that he wanted to kill himself. Thankfully, her brother asked for help. He asked Brooke's husband to take him to treatment, and he went and got sober. He's been sober for over 14 years today. Brooke also has a sister, who thankfully did not suffer from addiction.

At home, Brooke's immediate family wasn't exempt either. Her oldest son moved out and got married. Her two other sons, ages 18 and 15 at the time, starting drinking and using pretty heavily.

Her middle son, the 18-year-old, was doing incredibly well in school and earned straight-As until suddenly he stopped going to school and started hanging out with the wrong people. He was getting into trouble, getting arrested. Brooke felt so much shame. Her son was supposed to be graduating in a month, and instead, he became homeless. She found support at AA and Al-Anon meetings where other parents had experienced similar situations. She wasn't alone, and she had other parents that she could talk to about it. He was in and out of jail for months; Brooke or her ex-husband would bail him out, and he would go right back to what he was doing before.

Eventually, Brooke learned the value of saying "no" to her addicted son. She would no longer bail him out or enable him. It was an incredibly brave thing for Brooke to do. Saying "yes" would have been easier. One day when her son had been arrested again, he phoned Brooke, crying and begging for her to get him out, but she said no. Her son called her ex-husband, his father, and he also said no. That same day, his dad had a heart attack and died.

Eventually, Brooke did get him out of jail to attend treatment, but after six months, he went back to drinking and using. He went to prison for two and a half years after that, and Brooke was grateful that she was sober so that she could support and visit him there. In prison, her son got a sponsor and did the steps of the AA (Alcoholics Anonymous) and NA (Narcotics

Anonymous) programs. When he left prison, he was two and a half years without drugs and alcohol. While in prison, he got his GED. And afterward, he attended university where he graduated top of his class. He also met his wife in recovery. Looking back, Brooke is proud of how far her middle son has come and how different his life looked at 21 after his jail term versus 18 when he was getting into alcohol and drugs. He and his wife now have four children.

Her youngest son also got into recovery and is currently over 17 years off drugs and sober. He is married with a family. Her oldest son ended up getting a divorce from his wife, who suffered from alcoholism.

Brooke lost her father after a battle with cancer at 80 years old. Seven years later, she lost her mother. The end-of-life process was hard, Brooke recalls. There was selling her home, moving her into a care center, and all of those sorts of tasks. Her husband's mother also passed away at 74 years old from cancer. She had been part of the AA program and knew Brooke's brothers too.

Brooke feels shame at so many points in her life, but the key to her sobriety is accepting and moving forward. She felt shame because her son was so close to graduation and landed in prison. She felt shame that she would leave joints in the ashtray or bottles of tequila on the table when the kids were younger. She felt shame that she couldn't remember if she had nursed her son. She felt shame when she would leave work for lunch, have a few drinks, and return with alcohol on her breath. She felt like she couldn't share what happened behind closed doors because the stigma was so great. What would people think? They certainly wouldn't understand.

When I spoke with Brooke, she was turning 70 years old the very next day. Her voice was full of joy, and her heart was full of gratitude for the life she gets to live every day. I wish there was a way I could convey that feeling onto paper so you could feel it too. She and her husband have a beautiful home and enjoy playing golf and providing service to others through meetings and sponsor activities. She attends AA and Al-Anon meetings to this day. Her home group meeting is at 6:45 AM every day. Brooke believes it is a great way to start the day.

Brooke's life has not been easy. Life isn't meant to be easy. It's meant to be lived. It's ugly, beautiful, tragic, and joyous all in one. It is what you chose it to be. I believe Brooke chooses to leave an impact each day through her family and service work. I hope you do the same.

Which brings us to Brooke's one thing: "There is support and love on the other side of addiction. Life can be amazing if we allow it to be."

Reflections

1. Brooke didn't feel like she was hurting anyone with her addiction. Take an honest look. Who are you hurting with your addiction?

2. Brooke didn't love herself. Once she learned to love herself, she didn't need to look to her father or then-husband for approval. She had it within herself all along. How can you show love to yourself?

3. As a Warrior in Recovery, Brooke learned the important and brave lesson of saying no. She couldn't save her kids just like her parents couldn't save her. Where can you learn to say no to the ones you love?

Don't forget that you can download the Warriors in Recovery companion workbook along with other bonuses and resources to help you on your journey by visiting www. melaniemoberg.com/warriorsinrecovery

EMILY

"Your first thought is always wrong. Think again."

Addiction does not discriminate. It doesn't look at one family and think, "Not this one, they make too much money" or "Not this one, they have a nice house." It simply doesn't work that way.

This next story has a special meaning to me. In listening to Emily tell her story, one person amongst all of the chaos and heartache stood out to me: her mother. Emily's mother wasn't struggling with addiction, but she was extremely codependent, just as I was. A codependent is someone whose life has become unmanageable as a result of having a relationship with an addiction issue. It can mean you want to help someone so badly that your own life suffers considerably. It means that you care so much that your needs and desires are pushed to the side so that you can "fix" the broken person.

If you've been around addiction long enough, you've likely learned that "fixing someone" is a recipe for disaster. Disaster not just for yourself but for the person you love. Disaster for the other people in your life outside of this codependent relationship. We cannot fix someone's addiction. We cannot throw money at it to make it go away. We cannot do the work for them. We must focus on ourselves and encourage and support them to do the same.

Emily's mother was a codependent. It began early in Emily's life when the family lived in a high-class neighborhood, her father, a successful doctor. Her parents had Emily attend a Catholic high school. One day, her guy friends got kicked out for rolling a joint in the gym. They quickly warned Emily that she was next. Emily phoned her mom and explained that she was about to get kicked out of school, so her mom called the school before they had a chance. Emily's mom told the school it was Emily's last day there and that she was switching to another school. After being saved from school expulsion, Emily went to a public school.

A few years prior, Emily had had her first taste of pot. She flew out to California to visit her best friend. They climbed up a mountain and smoked a joint together. Emily hadn't thought much of it. But when she returned home to New Jersey, she found herself hanging out with the wrong crowd. Not intentionally, but she was gravitating toward those people. She became a self-proclaimed "pothead." She also drank a lot with her friends in a small but nice town where a lot of drinking happened. Emily had grown up with money. She had the large house with the pool and the big screen, so everyone came to hang out at her house with her and her older siblings.

In every state, there are towns and neighborhoods that are just not good. They might have high crime, homelessness, and high drug use. As a senior, Emily had her driver's license, and she found one of these bad neighborhoods. There were so many drugs like mescaline, a psychedelic type of drug, and acid, new things for Emily to try. She was hanging out with drug dealers and people who had no problem selling crack to their own mothers. While Emily was experimenting with these new drugs, she still considered herself a pothead. It was her go-to.

One day, Emily was hanging out at a friend's house. Whenever they spent time there, they were supposed to stay in her friend's room, and anytime they were leaving, they had to knock and say, "Coming out!" so that the others in the house could have time to put away their drugs and such before they would see. On this day, Emily's friend left early, but she stayed at the house a while longer. She forgot to yell, "Coming out!" before she left his room, and when she opened the door, she saw her friend's mom at the kitchen table, smoking crack out of an asthma inhaler with a bunch of her friends. Not even 10 minutes later, Emily found herself carpet farming after trying it. Carpet farming is when a person is high and ends up on their hands and knees, looking at every speck on the floor or carpet in hopes that it might be a drug. It had hit Emily hard. She liked it and smoked it a few times, but was quickly cut off. Her friend had found out about it and wouldn't allow her to talk to his mom. Thankfully, Emily wasn't searching anywhere else for it because she didn't want to be called a crackhead.

During high school, Emily had been pulled over after just buying some pot in New York. There, she could buy it in bulk for cheap and bring it back to Jersey. But the cops didn't find the drugs, and Emily was free. Her car had no side mirrors on it because she was either so drunk or high that she would hit things and knock the mirrors off. Wrecking cars was a regular occurrence. Although Emily worked as a waitress at IHOP, she funded most of her drug use with money from her parents.

Emily's grades had never been great, and she didn't graduate. Her parents were determined to straighten her out, so they put her on a plane and sent her to live with her aunt in Mexico City. Emily's mom was back at it, trying to fix Emily any way she could. But in Mexico, Emily had freedom. She could get into clubs, she could drink, and she could smoke. Sure, she was only 17, but in Mexico, that part didn't matter. Her aunt knew all of this and would put a garbage can next to her bed and a two-liter soda so that when Emily woke up, she would have a place to vomit and a way to clean her mouth. Emily's aunt was so much like her mother. Like so many people, she cared greatly and wanted to take care of Emily.

Eventually, Emily left Mexico and returned to New Jersey to pack up and move to San Francisco. It was there that Emily attended an art school, hoping to become a fashion illustrator. School proved a challenge for Emily. She wasn't sober so drawing what she was seeing wasn't cutting it, because she wasn't seeing straight. She was kicked out of classes and ultimately kicked out of school. She headed back to New Jersey.

Back home, Emily and another friend of hers needed to make

some money. One sure way to make fast cash was by stripping, so they walked into a bar with the intention of finding work stripping, but outside the bar were a couple of guys who asked the girls if they wanted to smoke some pot together. They became instant friends. One of the guys Emily was talking to later became her boyfriend, but on this night, she was mostly interested in the drugs. The guys also asked if they had ever done coke, which Emily hadn't, but she was keen. The next day, she went to her dad's office in New York and asked him for money for clothes. He gave her $700, and Emily took it straight to Spanish Harlem.

Once there, Emily went in alone. She had no idea how much coke was a good amount, but she had $700 to spend, so she ended up with seven eight balls of cocaine. An eight ball is an eighth of an ounce of cocaine. That's a lot of cocaine. It was Emily's first time using it, and between her and five friends, it took a day and a half to get through. Emily didn't sleep for three days.

Finally, she slept, but when Emily woke up, her body wanted more. She could smell it in the air. She would do anything for more cocaine, so she stole her sister's safe and sold it. She later found out that her mom's five-carat platinum engagement ring was in there. She had asked for only $40.

It didn't stop with that safe. She stole and pawned her mom's china, and since she had the same first and last names, she could steal her mom's debit card and use it without anyone second-guessing her. Stealing from her family was acceptable in Emily's eyes, but she wouldn't steal from anyone else. Emily knew her mom wouldn't do anything about it. Although she didn't intend to be, Emily's mom was an enabler because there were no consequences for Emily when she stole from her mom.

Aside from stealing from her family, she had this relationship going on with the guy she met outside the bar. Before too long, she was pregnant. Emily had been really high for the two weeks before she knew she was pregnant, and she worried that she might have harmed the baby. Her mother gave her the option of terminating the pregnancy, but Emily was insistent that she would keep it. Her parents were divorced by now, so Emily had to drive to New York to tell her father. He asked his secretary to clear his calendar so that they could fly to Florida to take care of the issue. Emily's uncle was a surgeon in Florida, and her father seemed to think that the two of them would be able to perform the abortion. In his office, Emily and her dad screamed at each other, eventually so much so that his patients in the waiting room could overhear. Her dad let her go, but later, he drove to New Jersey, kicked her out of the house, and took her car away. She was literally barefoot and pregnant. He wouldn't let her get her shoes and had to call the police to have Emily escorted out because she refused to leave.

Emily had no choice but to live with her boyfriend. His mom was addicted to heroin and everyone in that house was using and high all the time. Emily stayed incredibly strong throughout that pregnancy and refused drugs for that time. Her focus was on her unborn baby. But they had no food or money. Emily's mom put some money on an account at a diner down the street so that she could eat, but her boyfriend would leave her in the apartment all day with no air conditioning or electricity. She was pregnant, hot, and hungry—a horrible combination. Emily thinks that her boyfriend was trying to keep her safe by keeping her in the apartment all day. Regardless, it wasn't a safe place for her to be. Eventually, Emily's mom came to pick her up.

Emily stayed off drugs and sober through her entire pregnancy and even through the first three months of her daughter's life while she nursed. After those three months, however, Emily began to smoke pot again and drink, but she really didn't do any other drugs. Then, a month later, when her daughter was four months old, Emily's mom decided that moving to Texas could help get Emily away from the people and environment that she knew in New Jersey. In her mom's eyes, it seemed that this might be the fresh start Emily needed.

She was 21 years old when they moved to Texas. She was drinking and smoking pot at the time, but it didn't take long for Emily's familiar life to catch up with her. She found the people she needed to get the drugs she wanted. Moving to Texas had the opposite effect to what her mom had hoped. Emily was no longer off drugs and sober. In fact, she was using more than she did in New Jersey. Back then, airport security wasn't what it is now. Emily would fly back to New Jersey from Texas with a straw and baggie of cocaine, sniffing on the airplane, pretending she had allergies with a tissue. She simply didn't care what people thought. She was ruthless.

From the outside, her life still looked pretty good. Emily always kept a job, usually waiting tables, and always had cocaine. Her friends joked about a cigarette pack where she kept her cocaine, which they dubbed the "Magic Newport Box" because they never knew how the cocaine got there, but it was always full. Emily wasn't having any major problems, but her mother was doing most of the work raising her daughter, as Emily simply wasn't capable. However, she was proud to be paying her bills. She was a weekend warrior.

Life took a drastic turn for Emily when her boyfriend back in New Jersey died. Within three days of being out of jail on some drug-related charges, he overdosed on heroin. Emily had pleaded with the family to keep him in jail, but they bailed him out.

Emily fell apart. She would leave the house and not come back for days because she'd be out doing drugs. She didn't want her daughter to see her that way, but inevitably she came home still drunk and sometimes even without her car. Her mom would ask, "Where's the car?" and Emily would simply shrug her shoulders and say, "I don't know."

During this time, Emily met a security guard. She wasn't interested in him at first, but once he mentioned that he had some ecstasy, she became intrigued. Emily and a friend of hers went to his house. It was a new beginning within a continual battle.

Emily was sad. She had lost her daughter's father. She felt alone and worried about the future. Even if her daughter's father wasn't around, being alive was still more than being dead. Now there was no chance for him to be in her daughter's life. This guy could cheer her up, make her feel better, take her worries away. All she had to do was hold a lighter under the foil and inhale through the straw. Crack. Meth. These became Emily's reason for living.

So, she dated this security guard and started stripping. It was easy money and meth had such a hold on her that she would do just about anything. She never prostituted herself, but she would bring girls to her drug dealer's house and prostitute them. She would get into cars with strangers and bring them into her house as long as they had drugs, and her mom and daughter were out of town. She was desperate, and while she had her limits, she was open to doing almost anything for drugs.

It became so bad that Emily's mom found a trustworthy guy to watch Emily when she was gone. He became Emily's best friend, like a brother to her. He had never used drugs and treated her like a little sister. Emily's mom would call him when she went out of town and say, "Please babysit her. I don't want her to be dead when I get home."

Throughout all of this, Emily's security guard boyfriend got arrested on some drug charges and was sentenced to mandatory rehab. He called Emily from rehab and told her that he couldn't talk as long as she was still using.

So, somewhat suddenly, this person she found solace in, this person who made her feel less sad and worried was gone. It didn't take long for Emily to find that same feeling in another person. It wasn't about the personality. It was about a physical presence. Her drug dealer's nephew fit the bill, and he soon moved in with Emily, her mom, and daughter. Since this guy was related to her dealer, it meant that Emily was part of the family and didn't have to pay for drugs anymore.

Emily continued to use for a while and then realized how lonely she had become; she didn't want to do this anymore. She called a friend that she knew had found recovery and asked him how he had done it. He asked Emily if she had any drugs on her, and she responded with, "Yeah. Duh." He told her to throw them out, but Emily couldn't do it. She wasn't quite ready to quit. He told Emily, "Call me when you're done because you're not done.".

A few days passed, and it was her daughter's sixth birthday. Emily was supposed to be at Chuck E. Cheese for the birthday party, but she had got so messed up the night before that she couldn't even find her clothes to get dressed. She showed up at the party in overalls with her stripper dress underneath and stripper heels, because she had lost her sneakers somewhere. At first, Emily was proud that she'd made it at all, but she noticed pretty quickly that people were staring at her. She certainly didn't look like she belonged at Chuck E. Cheese. The one person who really mattered that day, her daughter, didn't notice anything unusual about her mom's appearance, though. To her daughter, Emily looked like Mom. In that moment, Emily realized that her daughter thought that is what Mom looked like all the time.

The shame of that day sent Emily into a tailspin. Emily took some GHB that resulted in a two-day blackout that she doesn't remember at all. While she was still high, she picked up the phone and called her friend, the same friend who'd told her she wasn't ready. Emily wanted help. He told her that his sponsor wouldn't let him take her to a meeting because she was not sober, and they had used together in the past. However, he told her where the meeting was.

That was March 16, 2003.

When her mom took her to that meeting with her daughter, Emily struggled to step out of the car. She felt like she was losing her best friend: the drugs. She couldn't figure out how she could do this, but she was determined. Finally, her daughter asked, "Do you need me to walk you in?" That was the push Emily needed to get out of the car.

Emily's friend had told some of the members that Emily would be coming that night, so when she arrived, there were some strangers outside who knew her name and were trying to be friendly. They reached out to hug her and touch her, and Emily just couldn't understand why these people were being so nice to her. She was having a hard detox: screaming and burning, still in pain 48 hours later, on the floor, spitting on herself, drooling, crying and sweating, just miserable. She arrived wearing pajamas with bulldogs on them, covered in snot, spit, and sweat. And yet, these people were still hugging her.

She didn't really trust that this way of life was for her. She didn't think that hanging out at these meetings was going to help her have a real life suddenly, but she continued attending anyway. Her newfound sobriety was threatening to her boyfriend, who still lived in her house and was actively using. But Emily held strong and committed to her new path. She stayed sober and didn't use drugs.

No one knew this version of Emily. For most of her life, she had been addicted to drugs and alcohol. There was no history for her mom to know how to handle her this way. Her mother became really confused, and within 10 days of Emily's sobriety, her mom kicked her out of the house for two days. Emily was angry and mean. She had wanted the keys to her mom's car, and when her mom had refused, Emily had kicked a hole in the wall. All of the emotions that Emily had worked so hard to numb with drugs were coming to the surface.

At the Narcotics Anonymous (NA) meetings, Emily was spending time with new people, who were sober and not using drugs, and seemed to care about her. One of those people, Troy, quickly became one of her favorite people.

All the while, Emily was continuing to date the drug dealer's nephew. Sometime in August, Emily began to feel unwell. Her body had started to work properly again, and she had become pregnant with this guy's child. When she told him about the pregnancy, the boyfriend claimed it must be some other guy's baby, and it wasn't his. He left. He called her only once after that. All she said to him was: "I found your stash in my house, and I flushed it. And before I flushed it, I threw up on it from the morning sickness from 'not your baby.'" She had a healthy baby boy.

While Emily wasn't religious about completing her steps, she did what worked for her. It seemed that sobriety was in the bag. She had a good two years of recovery when she met her husband on MySpace, an old social network online. She enjoyed the messages and conversations they would have, but never expected it to go anywhere. However, he had a daughter too and wasn't scared of Emily's situation. They met 15 days after their first conversation on MySpace and married within the year.

A few years later, Emily received a dreadful phone call. Her close friend Troy who she'd met at NA had been found dead in a hotel room. Troy was adopted and having health problems. He was also diabetic and unbeknown to his friends and family, Troy was in kidney failure. Troy had found his birth mom and called her house, but her husband answered the call and said, "I know exactly who you are. Leave us alone." Apparently, his birth mom had had an affair, and when Troy was born as a result of that affair, he was not welcome in their family and given up for adoption. On being rejected again by his birth family, Troy had cleaned out his apartment, put all his affairs in order, locked his insulin in a hot car, and gone up to his hotel room. Then he got high and fell into a diabetic coma. When they found him, he was reaching for the phone. Emily believes he had changed his mind about killing himself, but it was too late. Troy was gone.

After the news about Troy, Emily started drinking. She didn't consider it a relapse, because she felt she had it under control. Her NA community felt she should reestablish, but Emily stayed grounded in her position.

Then she found out she was pregnant. She quit drinking, and life seemed normal. She felt like she was cured and had it all figured out. She had another healthy baby boy, but after the birth, she started drinking again. She doesn't know why, but in her own words, Emily says she went "crazy," kicked out her husband, and wanted a divorce. It didn't make sense. There was no other reason for this to happen than her "gremlin," what she calls her addiction, surfacing again, and wanting back in her life. That gremlin was part prison and part freedom. Emily was caught between it all, being yanked around like she was on some rubber band loop, never really sure where she was going to land.

She got back together with her husband, but her drinking

was still out of control. They would go to friends' houses, and she would down shots of alcohol, then head into the bathroom to get sick. Her husband would be waiting for her, knowing that he would have to clean up the mess she left behind.

Throughout all of this, Emily's daughter always lived with Emily's mother, while Emily and her husband had the boys and lived 15 minutes away. Then one day, when her daughter was 15, Emily got a phone call from her daughter's school saying that she had been cutting herself. Emily went to her mom's house to talk with her and said, "You told me you could do this better than me." It upset her daughter, and she refused to talk to Emily, but they were able to get her admitted to a therapy school where she could attend treatment sessions in the morning and classes in the afternoon.

One of her daughter's friends from her old school confided in a teacher that Emily's daughter had a private Instagram page where she shared her anorexia and self-harm journey. It was common for her daughter to punch herself and bruise her face. She cut herself and beat herself up, and others watching would comment saying they wished they could cut that deep and wondered how she could go so long without eating, as if it were a good thing. On the day that the friend said something, it was because Emily's daughter had posted, "This is the day I'm going to kill myself." The next day, they committed her daughter to a mental health program.

That night, Emily got incredibly drunk. That was over five years ago today, and Emily hasn't had a drink since. She was either going to become a raging alcoholic and lose everything or she was going to sober up and grow up because her daughter needed her. Emily's daughter has her own addiction story, and Emily is open with her kids about addiction because it is a genetic disease. She warns them to be careful.

Emily isn't active with meetings, but she will go to a meeting if the desire arises or if she can smell cocaine in the air. She mostly depends on her family as her recovery.

Which brings us to Emily's one thing: "Your first thought is wrong." Essentially, emotions can be dangerous. Sometimes, taking a few minutes, hours, or even days to consider what you want to do is an important step. So, before you make a decision, take some time to think over the consequences. Perhaps your first thought is wrong. Maybe the second or third thought is the best one. Go on a walk or run, clear your head, and then make a decision.

Reflections

1. Emily's mother was like many mothers with children who struggle with addiction. She wanted to help. Do you have someone like this in your life, or are you like this with people you love? What can you do differently?

2. After her daughter's birthday party, Emily got really high because of how ashamed she was. When have you felt shame? How did you manage it? What is one healthy way you can cope with strong feelings?

3. As a Warrior in Recovery, Emily knew she wanted to find recovery for a while before she was able to step into it. How can you support a sober lifestyle for yourself or a loved one?

Don't forget that you can download the Warriors in Recovery companion workbook along with other bonuses and resources to help you on your journey by visiting www. melaniemoberg.com/warriorsinrecovery

FINAL THOUGHTS

I learned so much while listening to these women tell their stories and writing this book. I hope you've found some of it helpful to you on your journey as well. One of the best ways to understand people is to listen to them. I am so grateful for these women sharing their stories so that I could better understand addiction and mental health.

I live in a small town about 40 miles west of the Twin Cities in Minnesota. Growing up, anytime we'd venture off to the big city, I would always look out the car window when we reached an exit, where there would usually be a homeless person holding a sign, asking for money. As I've grown up, my thoughts on what a person does when you see someone asking for help has changed greatly. In all honesty, when I was younger, it was quite scary to see people on the street corners asking for help. I was pretty accustomed to living in a small town where I knew every person. There were no homeless people to my knowledge. If there were, everyone in town would've known about it because it would've been the conversation at the local diner where I worked. As I grew older, seeing homeless people became even more uncomfortable. The thoughts went something like:

- "I mean, get a job. Go find work."
- "Why should I work hard for my money and give it to you?"
- "You are sitting on the street corner while you could be working."
- "What a worthless person using our resources."

Pretty crappy, right? I feel like shit for ever thinking that way. I'm happy to say that my thoughts shifted pretty quickly. My brother had an incredibly kind heart, and although he didn't have wealth, he was an extremely giving person. When he saw the homeless man on the corner, he gave him money. He didn't look the other way because he was uncomfortable. He opened his heart and helped the man.

We've all heard stories of people that stand on the street corners with their Mercedes parked around the corner. But let me tell you, now when I see a person asking for help, I do not turn my head because it makes me uncomfortable. I will help.

Yes, it might be a scam. There might be a Mercedes around the corner. But there might be a family that needs your help. This person might need something to eat. It might be the only thing they have eaten for days. So, from now on, I vow to help.

This is one amazing gift that I have received from this book, among countless others. My ability to see beyond the surface has grown leaps and bounds. I have empathy where I didn't before. I also know that throughout these stories, women recovered by doing three things:

- They found connection.
- They learned to be true to themselves.
- They asked for help.

CONNECTION

Connection is incredibly important. Everyone suffering from addiction suffers from loneliness. Either because they are isolating themselves or they feel that they are alone even though there may be several people in their everyday life. Courtney, the woman that became addicted to Adderall in college, felt lonely. She didn't have many friends and had moved away from her family to attend college. She lacked connection. But she wasn't the only one. Each of the women in these stories felt lonely in some way. When they were able to find a way to connect again, it made a world of difference.

Courtney was able to find connection by joining a CrossFit gym. It was a competitive environment centered around fitness, which were both things that were important to Courtney. Other women found connection in 12-step groups. Sarah found connection at a moms' recovery group. Brenda found a spiritual connection that made a difference.

It doesn't matter how you connect. It only matters that you connect with something or someone that resonates with you. For some people, that will be a 12-step group or different kind of recovery group. It might be a running club, church, or book club. Find what speaks to you and see if it fills you up.

A few years back, I was serving on my church's council as the treasurer. At first, I really enjoyed it. I looked forward to the meetings and seeing the people there. I liked the work we were doing. After some time, however, it became draining. I dreaded going. I no longer looked forward to those monthly Tuesday night meetings, so I resigned.

You can do that too. If something is no longer serving you, you can walk away. There is no contract binding you to be part of a club you no longer enjoy. If you aren't genuinely excited about what you've chosen for connection, then try something else. I promise your thing or your person is out there.

BEING YOURSELF

Maybe you have thought to yourself:

- "If they knew what I did when no one was looking, they wouldn't like me at all!"
- "No one understands me."
- "I have to look a certain way."
- "I don't fit in."

Perfectionists, sit down for this. No longer do we have to behave a certain way, dress a certain way, or wear our hair a certain way. If you are female and want to shave half your head and leave the other half long, that is now trendy! It's called a pixie cut. Totally acceptable! Cool, even.

Afraid that someone won't like the real you? I get it. I got an accounting degree because I thought I would make good money and always have a job. Both are true. But what I learned is that a job is not at all what I want. I want to look forward to every single day. I began to save money, and as I did, I've been slowly stepping away from that accounting job and doing what I love, helping people with mental health and addiction. It fills me up. It may take away most of the security I thought I wanted, but I did it anyway. It took me years. Years. And all the while, I was building my coaching practice, still constantly worrying about what people think. Would they judge my stories? Would they judge me? One day, I realized my happiness was more important than what someone else might think.

Today, I (mostly—still working on it!) post to social media and my blog without any filter. Sometimes I hit the "post" button and pee myself a little. Still, I do it. It won't be easy. It will take some practice. Just promise me this … Don't wait years. Do it today!

Cindy spent a large chunk of her life trying to be someone she wasn't. Her mother's thoughts for who Cindy should have been are simply heartbreaking. I can't imagine the pain she felt every day, knowing she was different and not able to be herself. Brenda spent years trying to be the perfect woman. She wore the heels, she looked the part, and she had a great career. Behind closed doors, Brenda couldn't keep it up. None of these women could keep it up. It's not possible.

God made you exactly who and what you are for a reason. The world needs that version of you. The real deal. He didn't make you the type of person who would stand quietly by when your heart wants you to speak. He made you to stand up for what you believe in. Be you. There is no one better for that job. You deserve that feeling of freedom.

If your mother or your husband doesn't approve, that's okay. No approval from anyone is necessary to be yourself. Refer back to the chapter on self-love. And then re-read it. Freedom can be yours.

ASKING FOR HELP

Most people who know me would probably laugh that I am putting this as a recommendation. I am notoriously shitty at asking for help. But hear me out. I have asked for help from time to time, and when I am open to receiving it, help makes a world of difference. Help can take several forms:

- A friend or family member
- A counselor or therapist
- A spouse or significant other
- A colleague
- A journal
- A higher power (God, prayer)

Sometimes, we don't need anyone to take the wheel. Sometimes, we just need someone to listen. I never knew what it was like to have someone just listen and care about what I had to say for an hour. I never knew that I needed someone to listen to me like that. I took a chance on seeing a therapist, and it made a huge difference in my life. In between therapy appointments, I found journaling and prayer to be super helpful. I also had two girlfriends who I confided in about *everything*. I was blessed, to say the least. Not everyone has one person that they feel comfortable talking to, let alone two. Find someone or something. Pray to God like he is sitting by your side, holding your hand.

(He is, by the way.) Journal like you are writing your imaginary best friend a letter about it. Find a counselor you like. You might not get it right on the first or second appointments. Keep trying until you find someone that jives with you.

Freedom found her help in the back of a cop car that brought her to jail, Brooke found help at a 12-step meeting, and Kayla found help in a CPS agent. It doesn't matter who or what, just lean into the help when it presents itself. That is a light moment, and what we do in these moments matters.

I can't tell you that if you make some changes life will be magical and better overnight. I wish I could. It simply doesn't work that way. Life was never meant to be easy. It was meant to challenge us, make us angry, sad, and hopeless—all to lift us back up the next day.

After my brother passed away, an aunt suggested that I visit a medium. She had a son pass away and couldn't believe how accurate her reading was. So, a complete sucker for this sort of thing, I said, "Hell yes!" and booked an appointment. I was blown away by what I learned and how I felt my brother's hands—quite literally—touching me. If you are open to a new experience, I suggest finding a reputable medium and having a session. When I had this session, I was newly separated and miserable. My brother had killed himself, I was getting divorced, and I had two young kids. To sum it up: I felt pretty damn hopeless. Life sucked, and I didn't understand why crap kept happening to me.

At this session with the medium, she said to me (on behalf of my brother), "Melanie, life was never meant to be easy."

Life was never meant to be easy. This coming from my brother who had killed himself. What incredible insight. When she first told me this, I had to admit I felt embarrassed and ashamed for feeling so sorry for myself. I was alive. No one would deny that I was in a hard time, but that's all it was—a hard time. Anytime I feel down or hopeless, I remember these words, and I know that a better day is around the corner. Your better day is coming, too.

BONUSES

Head on over to www.melaniemoberg.com/warriorsinrecovery for some fun bonuses and useful resources to help you on your journey!

Stay connected by joining us on Facebook:
https://www.facebook.com/melaniemobergcoach

Join our online community here:
https://www.facebook.com/groups/peacewithinme

ACKNOWLEDGEMENTS

To the women who trusted me to share their stories, thank you. I learned so much in the process of gathering your stories and this book would not have been possible without your contribution. I am blessed to have heard your story first-hand and am honored to be trusted with sharing it. I hope this book reminds you of your courage, your strength, and your resilience. You are providing inspiration and hope to women every day. You've left an imprint on my heart and I am forever grateful for you.

I also want to thank my friends and family, especially my kids, Ryan and Emily, and my niece, Brianna. Throughout this project, you were selfless with sharing your time. Your love and encouragement helped me cross the finish line. I will always work to show you what is possible when your priority is helping others. To my parents, thank you for not always understanding what I am up to, but rolling with it anyway! Your support is one thing I can always count on.

I was also blessed to find Annick Ina, book doula extraordinaire, when I felt like setting this whole project aside, yet wanted to give these stories a home. Your encouragement and coaching helped me stay accountable to these stories and bring them to life. You also led me to my amazing editor, Kris Emery. Thank you, Kris, for making this book the best possible version it could be. Your feedback and suggestions were priceless. I am incredibly grateful to have such a great team behind this book.

ABOUT THE AUTHOR

Melanie Moberg is a Codependency Coach, helping her clients navigate the difficulties of loving someone suffering from mental health or addiction issues, often at the cost of their own well-being.

Melanie has an array of experience with mental health and addiction as several people in her life suffered or continue to suffer with addiction and mental health issues. When her brother Michael took his life in 2013 while he was drunk and high, Melanie set out on a path determined to create change.

She earned her Master of Arts degree in *Addiction Counseling: Integrated Recovery for Co-Occurring Disorders* from Hazelden Betty Ford Graduate School of Addiction Studies and uses that knowledge to advocate for mental health and addiction recovery every day.

REFERENCES

National Institute of Mental Health (NIMH). (n.d.). Substance Use and Mental Health. Retrieved from https://www.nimh.nih.gov/health/topics/substance-use-and-mental-health/index.shtml

Pompili, M., Serafini, G., Innamorati, M., Dominici, G., Ferracuti, S., Kotzalidis, G. D., Serra, G., Girardi, P., Janiri, L., Tatarelli, R., Sher, L., & Lester, D. (2010). Suicidal behavior and alcohol abuse. *International journal of environmental research and public health*, 7(4), 1392–1431. https://doi.org/10.3390/ijerph7041392

RESOURCES

Suicide Prevention Hotline
Call 1-800-273-8255
https://suicidepreventionlifeline.org/

Crisis Text Line
Text 741741
https://www.crisistextline.org/

National Domestic Violence Hotline
Call 1-800-799-7233
Text LOVEIS to 22522

Melanie Moberg, Codependency Coach
www.melaniemoberg.com

Smart Recovery
https://www.smartrecovery.org/

NAMI (National Alliance on Mental Illness)
https://nami.org/

Alcoholics Anonymous
https://www.aa.org/

Al-Anon
https://al-anon.org/